Donna Raymond

"When I die, my epitaph or whatever you call those signs on gravestones is going to read: 'I joked about every prominent man of my time, but I never met a man I didn't like! I am so proud of that I can hardly wait to die so it can be carved. And when you come to my grave you will find me sitting there, proudly reading it."

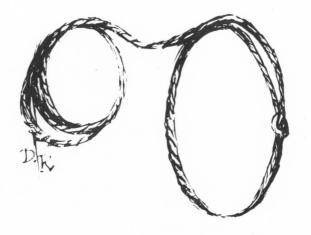

D. RAYMOND

Will Rogers
COOKBOOK
REVISED EDITION

EDITOR: DONNA RAYMOND
ARTWORK, COVER: DON P. RAYMOND

---

with the sayings of Will Rogers

---

*Will Rogers Cooperative Association
of Will Rogers State Historic Park
Pacific Palisades, California*

Photographs

Family pictures, Will and Betty and children Will, Jr., James and Mary– pp. 16, 205

Will Rogers – pp. 24, 104, 135, 151, 159, 167, 179, 180, 192, 194, 225, 272

Scenes at the Pacific Palisades home – pp, 136, 160, 205

Will with his sister Sallie McSpadden and her husband Tom – p. 22

Joel McCrea – p. 26

Buddy Rogers and Mary Pickford – p. 127

With Mary Carlisle in "Handy Andy"– p. 152

With Anne Shirley in "Steamboat Round the Bend"– p. 152

With Billie Burke in "Doubting Thomas"– p. 168

With Ivan Lebedeff and Andre Cheron in "A Connecticut Yankee"– p. 168

With son Jimmy – p. 180

Typing newspaper article at the movie lot – p. 194

Soapsuds – Will's horse – p. 224

At Chicago, Republican National Convention, 1932 – p. 272

WILL ROGERS COOKBOOK – REVISED EDITION

Copyright © 1992 Will Rogers Cooperative Association
> *A non-profit organization of docents who are dedicated to keeping the memory of Will Rogers alive for all America to enjoy.*

Printed in the United States of America

Credits
Art – Don Raymond
Pictures – from the archives of Will Rogers State Historic Park, Pacific Palisades, California.
Quotes – Will's sayings throughout this book are used with permission of Joseph Carter.
Director of Will Rogers Memorial, Claremore, Oklahoma.
Typesetting and printing – Chicago Printing and Embossing Company

DEDICATED TO THE MEMORY
OF WILL ROGERS
AND TO
BRYAN AND FRANCES STERLING FOR THEIR
DEDICATION TO THE MEMORY OF WILL
ROGERS

"When you have helped to raise the standard of cooking, you have helped to raise the only thing in the world that really matters anyhow. We only have one or two wars a lifetime, but we have three meals a day."

Will Rogers

ACKNOWLEDGMENT

This revised edition of the Will Rogers Centennial Cookbook has had a great response from new docents, park people,and many new friends. Thank you to all who so generously shared their prize recipes.

Thank you to Joseph H. Carter, director of the Will Rogers Memorial, in Claremore Oklahoma, for permission to use the Will Rogers quotations throughout the cookbook.

Thank you to Bryan and Frances Sterling for their devotion to the memory of Will Rogers and their help in obtaining special recipes.

The cookbook committee, Docent President, Gene Asanovich, Harriet Axelrad, Marjorie Hanson, Trudy and Emil Sandmeier, gave me a lot of support, thank you all. A special thank you to Trudy Sandmeier, for her love, friendship and understanding, in compiling this cookbook.

A special thank you to my husband Don, for his artwork throughout the cookbook and also the cover design.

Donna Raymond—Editor

BIOGRAPHY–WILL ROGERS
NOVEMBER 4, 1879
AUGUST 15, 1935

"There was something neighborly about him," Mrs. Rogers wrote in loving remembrances of Will, "something that made you feel as though you had always known him."

It was this something that secured a permanent place for Will Rogers in the hearts of the American people. To them he was more than an actor, humorist, or journalist. He was their spokesman, the voice of the 1920s and 1930s, the conscience of America.

He won the love and respect of his countrymen with his great humanity and his jovial but pointed commentaries on the political abuses and social inequities in the national affairs of his time.

The sound wisdom behind his barbs, his genial nature and the sparkling freshness of his humor endeared him even to those who were his favorite targets. To be the subject of Will's satire was a sort of status symbol. His shrewd wit was completely without bitterness and was amicably aimed at the foibles and follies of bigwigs and to protest whatever encroached upon the rights and welfare of the people. In so doing he made the whole world laugh.

Will was born William Penn Adair Rogers on November 4, 1879, in Indian Territory, now the State of Oklahoma. Both parents were of partial American Indian ancestry through the Cherokees. Scotch-Irish forebears had married into the tribe on the father's side, and Dutch and Welsh on the mother's.

Will was the youngest of four surviving children in a family of eight. His father, Clement Vann Rogers, was an enterprising, ambitious and independently wealthy cattleman and rancher. Rogers County was named for Clem Rogers and was the district he represented in the constitutional convention which resulted in statehood for Oklahoma.

Will's mother, nee Mary America Schrimsher, bestowed upon her only surviving son a gentle love and a marvelous sense of humor, two gifts which remained with him throughout his lifetime. Her death when he was ten years old was a traumatic experience for the young boy.

Young Will was given every advantage in order that he might be encouraged to follow in his father's footsteps. But he had one great love the lariat, which, along with his sense of humor, brought the wrath of his teachers down upon him, but which eventually led to fame, fortune and world acclaim.

Will's career began in Wild West shows. His cowboy roping and riding acts carried him around the world and finally to New York City and the theatrical circuits of the early 1900s. By 1915 he had reached the top in vaudeville. His roping skill and incisive wit made him the featured attraction at the famous Palace Theater in New York City. Shortly after, he became a part of the Midnight Frolic on the roof of the New Amsterdam Theater and later joined the Follies of Florenz Ziegfeld, Jr. From there he moved upward into silent films and on to Hollywood, California in 1919.

Will's experience in silent films was disappointing and without any lasting success, as was a temporary venture he made into producing silents on his own. He found it financially necessary in 1921 to return for a time to the Follies.

At this time he began to develop and use his talents as a banquet speaker, lecturer, newspaper columnist and later as a radio commentator. Through these media, especially his newspaper columns, more than through his films, Americans learned to love him, and his name became a household word.

Will's weekly column first appeared in the New York Times in December, 1922, and was soon syndicated. Four years later his Daily Telegram, a commentary on world affairs, was initiated and syndicated as "Will Rogers Says . . ." It eventually became a feature in more than 500 newspapers in the U.S.

Film stardom came to Will with the advent of talking pictures. His first "talkie" was made in 1929, when he was almost 50 years old, and by 1933 he and Marie Dressler were the top box-office attractions. A year later he was at the top by himself, and at the time of his death, he was still the leading attraction along with Shirley Temple.

Of his marriage to Betty Blake in 1908, Will said, "The day I roped Betty I did the star performance of my life." Mrs. Rogers was the guiding factor and stabilizing influence in Will's life and career. She recognized his genius and unselfishly devoted her time and efforts, her life, in support of him. She was his companion and mentor during their life together. Three sons and a daughter were born to them. The youngest child, Freddie, died in 1920 in Hollywood.

After Freddie's death and until 1927, the Rogers lived in Beverly Hills. In 1928 they moved to their Santa Monica ranch which was Will's home for the last seven years of his life.

On August 15, 1935, a tragic airplane crash in Alaska took the life of Will and of his friend, the famous pilot, Wiley Post. Will's untimely death at the peak of his career confirmed his status as a national folk hero. His own words, spoken many years before, simplistic as they were, seemed strangely prophetic: "This thing of being a hero, about the main thing to it is to know when to die."

Will was the living embodiment of the philosophy of individual freedom, social equality and the natural goodness of man. He lived this philosophy in his associations with others, both the humble and the great. He was a friend of the poor, of kings and princes, men of letters, the great leaders of the world. Four American presidents welcomed him to the White House during their respective administrations. They were Warren Harding, Calvin Coolidge, Herbert Hoover and Franklin Roosevelt. For them he was America's Ambassador of good will.

His ranch home in Pacific Palisades, now Will Rogers State Historic Park, is a repository of memorabilia of his life. They are reminders of his human relationships, his pride in his Cherokee background, his homely philosophy and the simple virtues that shaped his character kindness, honesty, humor, generosity and love.

WILL ROGERS

A "ropin' fool" they called him,
This man one can't forget.
He walked with Kings and Princes
And liked each man he met.

He read the daily paper,
He said that's all he knew,
His homespun witty comments
Helped hone the public's view.

His gracious way of living
Included many guests
Who listened to his wisdom
And chuckled at his jests.

If you should come to visit,
To picnic, or to hike,
You'll find his ranch house open,
And that is what he'd like.

Though he's not there to greet you,
Just think that though he flew
To unknown lands far distant,
A welcome waits for you.

Harriet L. Axelrad
Will Rogers Docent

FOREWARD

A WILL ROGERS COOK BOOK? you may ask. Certainly, why not! If ever a man deserved to have a cook book printed in his honor, it was Will Rogers. After all, he had three basic prerequisites for such a tribute. First of all, as the owner of an operating spread in Oklahoma, he was a producer of food and interested in the future use - or abuse - of everything he sent to market.

Secondly, but probably foremost, Will Rogers was a consumer: "I am a fair eater," he admitted on his April 27, 1930, radio broadcast, "I don't eat correctly, but I eat a lot." Though a publicly confessed hardy eater, Will was neither a gourmet nor a gourmand. During his career he was feted at many an urbane banquet table; he was invited by magnates, millionaires and world leaders; he ate at the White House and he dined with nobility, yet he never developed an appetite for any of society's haute cuisine. It was not that he was unfamiliar with so-called sophisticated delicacies and international dishes; he had tasted most of them from caviar in Russia to bird's nest soup in China, from pheasant under glass in France to baked Alaska at the Waldorf-Astoria. In that respect he was unlike Tom Mix, the famous cowboy star. Mix, so it was reported, said after a dinner given in his honor at the Astor Hotel in New York City: "I et for two hours and didn't recognize a thing I et except an olive."

Despite the adulation of an era, despite riches and fame, despite familiarity with around-the-world cookery, Will Rogers' life and diet stayed rather basic. It has been said that you can take the boy out of the country, but you can't take the country out of the boy. Will Rogers, the world's first multi-media super-star, part cowboy, part Indian, lived his simple philosophy: "I am just an old country boy in a big town trying to get along. I have been eating pretty regular, and the reason I have been is because I have stayed an old country boy."

All his life Will's appetite remained loyal to the fare he first tasted on his parent's ranch in the Indian Territory that was to become the state of Oklahoma. Let's quote Will himself: "I love my navy beans better than any other dish, or half dozen dishes. Just old plain white navies, cooked in plenty of ham or fat meat, with plenty of soup among em. Not catsup or any of that stuff. Just beans and corn plain white navies, cooked in plenty of ham or fat meat, with plenty of soup among em. Not catsup or any of that stuff. Just beans and corn bread . . . and raw onions. Those three things are all I want."

Interviewing the great movie maker Hal Roach, Sr., some years ago, he recalled to us one of his favorite anecdotes which showed that even Will's undying passion for beans had its limitation. Roach had been at the Rogers ranch in Pacific Palisades to play polo, and had been invited to stay for dinner. As usual, it was a sumptuous meal with plenty of good food and more than enough for at least another dozen guests, but no beans. It seems that Will, missing his favorite, complained to Mrs. Rogers: "Betty," so Hal Roach, Sr., recollected Will saying, "I want those Mexican beans every night." And this is how Hal Roach, Sr., remembered the events that followed: "The first night after that, Betty had a rather modest little dish prepared and Will said: 'Betty, that's not what I want. I love them. I want a lot of these beans.' Well, the next day, there was a bowl containing at least four quarts of beans sitting in front of Will. And for the next month, a bowl with four quarts of beans was in front of Will every night until he got so damn sick and tired of Mexican beans that he had to call it quits."

There is also no doubt about Will's addiction to chili, or "chili con carne, as you amateur eaters call it. I sure do love my chili," he wrote in his Weekly Article on July 17, 1927. It is told that Will would unhesitatingly eat in any restaurant which featured chili, whether it was a modest greasy spoon, or the famous Dinty Moore's off Times Square in New York City. In fact, when in Manhattan, Dinty Moore's was one of Will's favorite late night chili parlors. Often, after a show, while other performers would frequent the fashionable places of the moment to see and be seen, Will would sit at Dinty Moore's, joke with the patrons and eat his beloved chili.

In 1927, following Will Rogers' serious gall stone operation, he claimed "If I could have just bogged down to a few bowls of good old greasy chili, I would have been well in a week. But I got the next best thing that I wanted and that was some real corn bread." And Will even provided the recipe: "Not this old yellow kind made with eggs, but cornbread, real old corn dodger, corn pone made with meal, hot water and salt. . . But I had to have my sister, Mrs. Tom McSpadden from Chelsea, Oklahoma show 'em . . . how to fix some string beans with some fat meat. Not just boiled in old hydrant water, but a real piece of ham, or the side of a shoat . . . when the old appetite comes back you don t want to be mixed up with a kitchen where there is one of those dieticians, they know what is good for your health, but they don't know what is good for your appetite. They figure out the calories, but I like to figure out the odor. If I happen to be having some bean soup, I want to be able to locate, at pretty prompt intervals, some little objects that look to me like beans. I don't want a bowl of it where the beans have just been driven through there at low tide."

Signing his daily squib "Yours for corn bread, chitlins and turnip greens," he scoffed at a Californian's menu: "You give a Los Angelician . . . two hot dogs, a bottle of red soda pop, . . . and you have just about covered his national diet."

Let Will Rogers, himself, describe his perfect meal: "We always have such good things to eat at my sister's in Chelsea. Beans, and what beans, kinder soupy navy beans cooked with plenty of real fat meat. Well, when I can't knock off a whole bowl of those myself, why, I am sick before I start. And then the ham, fried ham; they cure their own ham. Tom McSpadden, my brother in law, he is the prize ham curer of any I ever saw. Smoked 'em with the old hickory fire, then salts 'em away for all this time."

"Then the cream gravy. You know there is an awful lot of folks that don't know much about eating gravy. Why, not to be raised on gravy would be like never going swimming in the creek. They got their own cows and real cream. Ham gravy is just about the last word in gravies. Course, good beefsteak gravy is good. You know, we fry our beefsteak. It's cut in thin pieces, and say, let me tell you something. Did you know all this eating raw, bloody, rare meat, like they order in these big hotels, and city people like, well, that's just them. That ain't old western folks. Ranch cooks and farm women fry steak thin and hard. That old raw junk goes for the high collars in cities, they are kinder cannibalistic, anyhow."

"Well, you can get some awful good gravy by putting your old milk in the skillet after you fried a lot of good beefsteak. There is an awful lot of good gravy! A good old home cook can mix up a tasty batch of gravy just about out of anything. No sir, the old city eaters missed some mighty fine grub when they don't take advantage of making gravy one of their regular dishes at every meal."

"Now then comes the corn bread . . . My old Daddy always had that at every meal, said it was only the high toned folks that eat biscuits, and light bread or loaves like you all eat now. He called that wasp nest, and thought that was just for the heathen. Well, this corn pone is mighty hard to go hungry after. You see, I am just a-telling you my dishes that they have when I come . . . they know I would rather have it than to go out and kill the fatted calf, or kill a turkey or some chicken."

"Then for desert? Don t have room for any desert. Had any more room, would eat some more beans."

And the third of Will Rogers distinction for having this book published in his name, is the fact that in 1929 he wrote the foreword to FASHIONS IN FOOD IN BEVERLY HILLS. It seems that the ladies of the Beverly Hill Women's Club decided to publish a cook book, and so they asked their famous 'ex-mayor' to write the introduction. Will explained the function of a cook book: "It's super cooking we are diagnosing for you in this gem of appetite. What am I doing in this book? I have the right of any wronged stomach to be here. I am here to assist my fellow man from having to eat some of the things that I have had to eat during the past. When you have raised the standard of cooking, you have helped to raise the only thing in the world that really matters, anyhow. We only have one or two wars in a lifetime, but we have three meals a day. There is nothing in the world we do as much as we do eating. Even sleeping don't start to compare with it. There is only one recipe for sound sleeping, that's a comfortable seat and a poor (motion) picture or a political speech."

"Now the little almanac of calories that follows will give you the ingredients of about all the different combinations that have been worked out with food as a background. Some of these were stumbled onto accidentally by reaching on the wrong shelf. A great many of the best ones in here were not premeditated. Cooking is a good deal like jokes, there are only seven original ones, and it takes a lot of scrambling em to get something that sounds or tastes different. To be a good cook, you got to be either naturally an experimenter, or just clumsy."

"The French have a reputation for good cooking, when it's only a reputation for camouflage, that they deserve. They can hide more through the sauce, your palate is in no mood to recognize the original goat meat hiding under the sauce. They can put a liquid overcoat, and non-pronounceable name, on a slice of horse meat and have an American wondering if it's breast of veal, or angel food cake." Will Rogers, Oklahoma food producer, consumer of hardy victuals and obvious authority on solid Western fare, would have liked this book; and he would have found his favorite dishes in these pages. It was left to the tireless efforts of Donna Raymond and the Docents of the Will Rogers Ranch in Pacific Palisades, California, to make the selections for this book. Every recipe has been kitchen-tested by Donna and judged by the Docents. Therefore Will Rogers quote from his foreword to the 1929 Beverly Hills Women s Club cookbook still holds:

". . .it's eating that keeps us here. So if these good ladies can help the world to better food, they will have performed a true service to everybody and a giant blow against indigestion."

Bryan and Frances Sterling.

ON COOKBOOKS AND COOKING
by Will Rogers

from the 1931 introduction to the
Beverly Hills Women's Club Cookbook

The Ladies (apparently) of the Beverly Hills Women's Club (yes, they got one), I don't belong to it, but it's here performing the usual function of all organized men or Women's Clubs, that is, trying to find something to do. Well these Ladies decided to get out a Cook Book. Now I don't know of a better place for a Cook Book to originate than in our City of Beverly Hills. For here the cooking is done by Cooks and not by Amateurs. Course there are a few local Wives that for pastime, or for the news reel Photographer, will dawn a Gingham creation, and detour to the kitchen, but this reign of indigestion in the family is only slight. The culinary Art returns to normal, and the Wife returns to her pursuit of love and happiness generally within a day's time.

So in that way we get good Cooking. You see this is an age of specialization. It's awful hard to be a good Cook and a loving helpmate. you can do the two, but one is apt to detract, one is bound to sooner or later suffer. There is bound to crop up a tinge of Ptomaine in the kitchen, or a slacking of helpmating in the rest of the home.

So we go out and get the best Cooks we can (well, we also go out and get the best Wives we can). But it's not wives we are discussing now, it's good Cooking. Course we got some mighty fine recipes in here by some of our most distinguished, and also lovely wives, but they only drew up the Blue Prints or ground plan. It's like an Architect. He tells you how to build a house, but did you ever see one he built for himself?

Now I don't mean by this that our Ladies can't cook as good as any other Wives anywhere else, for they can. But it's better cooking than that is what we are after, and that's our excuse for distributing this Pamphlet. Pretty near any woman can cook ordinary, (not only can but do,) but it's Super Cooking we are diagnosing for you in this Gem of Appetite. What am I doing in the book? I have the right of any wronged stomach to be here, I am here to assist my fellow man from having to eat some of the things that I have had to eat during the past. When you have helped to raise the standard of cooking, you have helped to raise the only thing in the world that really matters anyhow. We only have one or two Wars a lifetime, but we have three meals a day. There is nothing in the world that we do as much of as we do eating. Even sleeping don't start to compare with it. There is only one recipe for sound sleeping, that's a comfortable seat and a poor picture, or a political speech.

Now the little Almanac of calories that follows will give you the ingredients of about all the different combinations that have been worked out with food as a background. Some of these were stumbled onto accidentally by reaching on the wrong shelf. A great many of the best ones in here were not premeditated. Cooking is a good deal like Jokes . . . there are only seven original ones, and it takes a lot of scrambling 'em up to get something that sounds or tastes different. To be a good cook you got to be either naturally an experimenter, or just clumsy.

The French have a reputation for good cooking when it's only a reputation for Camaflouge that they deserve. They can hide more ordinary food under some kind of sauce, and by the time you dig through the sauce, your palate is in no mood to recognize the original Goat meat hiding under the sauce. They can put a liquid overcoat, and non-pronounceable name, on a slice of horse meat and have an American wondering if it's breast of veal, or Angel food cake. It's that gravy those Frogs pour on there that does the dirty work. They are just naturally sauce hounds. And over there the Government decorates men for dishing up food in such a way that no one knows what it is.

Cooking is not a necessity with them, it's an Art. And that's what these good Women of this Club (well, I guess we got maybe some good Women that are not in the Club), but it's the ones in the Club that I am telling you of now. I am just going to tell you "how to read the book" to get the most out of it. This is not an introduction; it's another recipe.

First you get hungry. This is no book for a satisfied stomach. The hungrier you get the better the book will appear. Naturally as you get hungry you start imagining, imagining what you would love to have to eat. When you get your mind set on just about what you would rather have than anything else in the World to eat why you turn to that particular page of the book where that particular type of food is advertised and there will be the prescription for that very dish that you have been craving to devour. Any kind of ration you can think of, some member of this Club thought of it before you did, cause we got plenty time out here to think, and you will find a plot of it right in this directory. Now I don't know how it's going to taste to you, for no two people have the same taste, and besides I don't know how you are going to mix it, no two people mix things the same. Tea cups are not always the same size, different hens lay different eggs, naturally. What you would call a "heaping teaspoon full" some stingy person might take for a saucer full. But if you follow the general directions in here you will land somewhere in the neighborhood of what our good Lady intended. If you haven't got all the ingredients, don't let that worry you. For in all these we have naturally allowed some leeway, and you can use something else. You won't get exactly what she was driving at, but you may get an improvement. Now take bread. I think it was H. G. Wells or maybe it was Brisbane who said, "Bread is the staff of life." Some of it is, and some is just an obituary notice. Now in here we tell you where to buy good bread. Study this little catalogue and meet your husband every week end when he drops in. Meet him with one of these prepared little antidotes, try 'em on him and then study him. There is an old Long Beach Proverb that reads, "The way to a man's stomach is through his eyes." Now we have some beautiful dishes in here, in fact some of 'em are better if you just make 'em and look at 'em, they are too good to eat. As I said before, eating is the biggest thing we have. you can talk disarmament, Ramsey Mac-Donald, Hoover's fishing, and all that, but it's eating that's keeping us here. So if these good Ladies can help the world to better food, they will have performed a true service to everybody and a giant blow against indigestion.

Will Rogers.

Reprinted from the Beverly Hills Women's club cookbook printed in 1931. Permission to use this introduction was given by Mrs. Herbert Olson, President.

CONTENTS

Biography of Will Rogers 7

Foreward, Bryan & Frances Sterling 11

On Cookbooks and Cooking, Will Rogers 17

Main Dishes 23

Casseroles 105

Salads 137

Sauces 153

Appetizers and Beverages 161

Soups 169

Breads 181

Desserts 193

Index 268

Main Dishes

Corned Beef and Cabbage a la Dinty Moore

Will Rogers, Jr.

Dad used to love to go to Dinty Moore's in New York for Corned Beef and Cabbage, and so did Florenz Ziegfeld. Mr. Ziegfeld had Dinty Moore send it to Palm Beach (by train in those days) for a dinner party he was having for 30 people.

Dinty Moore's was a favorite hangout of theatre people. It had spanking white tablecloths, mirrors above the dado rail and sawdust on the floor.

One of the Chefs from Dinty Moore's came up to cook at the Ziegfeld camp in Quebec, Canada. This is the way he made Corned Beef and Cabbage.

4 lb. piece of well-corned beef (brisket or round)
If only mildly corned add:
1 garlic clove
several whole pepper corns
bay leaf

Cover with boiling water and simmer 4 hours until a fork can penetrate to the center.

Wash and drain 1 or 2 heads firm cabbage cut in wedges; simmer on top of corned beef the last 15 minutes of cooking.

Serve with boiled white potatoes.

(About Food) "Know what's in it before you eat it."

Joel McCrea Recipe

I'm not much of a cook so my recipe won't amount to much. However anything to do with Will Rogers touches my heart–so here goes–

1 cup (large) beans
1 cup stewed tomatoes
1 sliced onion
3 eggs plus seasoning
Serve hot with sour dough toast.

Regards,
Joel McCrea

Note: Joel McCrea is the National Chairman of the Will Rogers Centennial Committee.

27

Estelle's Chicken Tortilla Especiale

4 c. chicken or turkey (bite-sized pieces)
12 corn tortillas, quartered
1/2 cup grated cheese
1 can cream of mushroom soup
1 cup evaporated milk
1 medium onion, grated
4 oz. green chile salsa

Mix last five ingredients together. Butter 9x13 pan. Put small amount of mixture in bottom of pan. Layer tortillas, chicken, and sauce mix. Repeat until all is used (sauce on top). Top with grated cheese. Let stand in refrigerator overnight. Bake at 300 degrees for one hour. Let stand out of oven for 10 or 15 minutes before serving. This serves ten people generously. It freezes well, but I recommend leaving off the cheese until ready to bake.

Gene Asanovich
Docent, Will Rogers State Park

"I have always maintaned that no president can be as bad as the men that advise him"

Sherried Chicken

1 Broiler-fryer, quartered
1/2 Cup butter or margarine
1 tsp salt
1/8 tsp pepper
1 Medium onion, thinly sliced
1/4 Cup tomato sauce
1/4 Cup sherry
1/2 Cup water

Season chicken with salt and pepper. In a large skillet heat butter or margarine, add chicken and saute until brown on all sides. Remove chicken and place in a single layer in a shallow pan, skin side down. Add onion to butter in skillet and saute until golden brown. Add tomato sauce, sherry and water, mix well. Pour half of sauce over chicken. Bake in a moderate oven for 30 minutes. Turn chicken and pour on remaining sauce. Continue baking thirty minutes longer, or until chicken is cooked, basting occasionally with pan liquid.

James Whitmore
Actor
Star of Will Rogers, U.S.A.

"The movie actors can't keep their mind on over one thing at a time, and that was How am I looking? And that is where the old stage always had it on the movies, you couldn't be a stage actor overnight. That had to come with years of experience. You got to do something beside being photographed on the old stage."

Family Pie

One handful of forgiveness,
One heaping cupful of love,
A full pound of unselfishness.
Mix together smoothly with complete Faith in God.
Add two tablespoons of wisdom,
One teaspoon of good nature for flavor,
Then sprinkle gently with thoughtfulness
and you'll have a never-fail Family Pie.

My name is Montie Montana, and one of the richest treasures of my lifetime, was knowing Will Rogers. Even today, after all of these years, I can set back and recount every single meeting, and each conversation I ever had with Will Rogers. He was that kind of man. Unforgettable! It is with great pride that I add my name to this book.

P.S. I'm not much of a "cook" but I believe anyone that follows this recipe, will find it a "never-fail."

Montie Montana

Crab Quiche

1 can crab
3 eggs
1/2 pint sour cream
1 cup shredded cheddar
1 tsp. salt
Dash tabasco
Pepper to taste
1 can French Fried Onions

Mix eggs well with sour cream. Add remaining ingredients, onions last. Put in greased pie tin. Bake 325 degrees for about one hour.

Irv Gordon
Docent, Will Rogers State Park

Paella Amigos

Serves 6

Lobster, cherrystone clams, mussels, olive oil, chicken, veal, lean pork, garlic, saffron, asparagus tips (fresh or canned), onion, salt, pepper, ripe tomatoes, rice, sweet red pepper, frozen peas, frozen artichoke hearts, crab meat, pimento.

SEAFOOD
Remove meat from: a 1-1/2 pound lobster. Scrub 6 cherrystone clams and 6 mussels. Pick over: 1/2 pound crabmeat.

MEAT
Cut into parts: 1 frying chicken. Dice 1/4 pound veal and 1/4 pound lean pork.

PAELLA
1. In a heavy deep skillet heat 1/4 cup olive oil.
2. Add chicken, veal and pork. Cook until chicken pieces are browned on all sides.
3. Add: 1 clove garlic, minced, and 1 onion, finely chopped. Cook, stirring, until onion is transparent.
4. Add: 2 teaspoons salt, 1/4 teaspoon freshly ground pepper, and 2 ripe tomatoes (1 pound), peeled and chopped. Cover and cook for 10 minutes longer.
5. Add: 2 cups rice and 4 cups water. Stir to combine.
6. Add: 1 sweet red pepper, chopped, 1 package frozen peas and 1 package frozen artichoke hearts. Cover and cook over low heat for about 20 minutes.
7. Mash in mortar: 1 clove garlic and 1 teaspoon saffron and add to paella. With large spoon turn rice from top to bottom to mix well.
8. Add the crabmeat and the lobster meat, cover, and cook for 10 to 15 minutes longer.

GARNISH: Meanwhile, put mussels and clams in a heavy pot with

1/2 cup water. Cover and bring to a lively boil over high heat. Cook for 2 minutes, or until shells open. Cook 12 asparagus tips until tender in boiling salted water (or heat canned asparagus).

PRESENTATION Arrange rice mixture in shallow paella dish or large shallow casserole. Place open mussels and clams in their shells on top of rice and garnish with the asparagus tips and strips of pimento.

Governor Jerry Brown

State of California

"California always did have one custom that they took serious . . . that was in calling everything a 'ranch'. Everything big enough to spread a double mattress on is called a 'ranch.'"

Karen Stouffer's Potato Supreme

3 medium potatoes
1 stick (1/4 pound) butter
1 envelope Lipton onion soup mix
1/4 Cup parmesan cheese
2 Tablespoons butter

Melt the butter in a two quart oven dish. Place the cleaned and thinley sliced potatoes in the melted butter, one layer at a time Sprinkle part of the onion mix over the potatoes, add the rest of the potatoes, and the rest of the onion soup mix. Spread the parmesan cheese over all. Dot with the butter.

Preheat the oven to 350°. Bake thirty minutes, check the potatoes. Cook until they are soft.

Donna Raymond
Docent, Will Rogers State Park

"The boy on the sand lot gets just as big a kick out of a home run as Babe Ruth did"

Wild Onion and Eggs American Indian Style

1 cup wild onions chopped
2 Tbls. bacon grease
3 eggs
1/2 cup water
Salt to taste

In a skillet, cook cleaned onions in bacon grease and water until done. Add salt and beaten eggs, stir often. Serve.

Some people like a lot of onions and just enough eggs to hold them together, others prefer more eggs scrambled with only a few onions for taste.

Wild onions are pulled in early spring, they grow in clumps, and are best when small, young and tender, but they are tedious to clean. The green is not all cut off, like green onions, it is edible as well as the nub, and while the top is thiner, they smell like onions.

Charles Banks Wilson
Artist, Lithographer, Muralist
Portrait Painter of Will Rogers
and Sequoyah.

D·R,

"I want to tell you right now it's the modern painter that has the tough job. He has to make 'em look enough like the millionaire wife so that the visitor can recognize her' and still make her look like she thinks she looks. When you can do that, then that's art."

Baked Snapper with Crab Meat, Mousseline Sauce

8 servings

Ingredients:
2 four-pound red snappers, cleaned and fileted (4 pieces)
1 pound lump crab meat
Salt
Pepper
3 teaspoons dried dill weed (or 3 tablespoons fresh chopped dill)
3 tablespoons lemon juice
12 tablespoons butter, melted (1-1/2 bars)

Preheat oven to 425 degrees

Instructions:
Place two fileted pieces of 2 four-pound red snappers in shallow oiled baking dish. Pick over 1 pound lump crab meat to remove cartilage and toss it gently with salt and pepper to taste, 3 teaspoons dried dill weed (or 3 tablespoons of freshly chopped dill), 3 tablespoons of lemon juice and 6 tablespoons of melted butter. Spread 1/2 crab meat mixture over pieces of snapper already in dish and cover with two remaining pieces. Secure with skewers. Pour remaining melted butter (6 tablespoons) over fish and bake for about 35 to 40 minutes in preheated 425 degree oven or until fish flakes easily. Arrange on warm serving platter. Remove skewers and garnish platter with crisp watercress or parsley as described. Serve with mousseline sauce.

MOUSSELINE SAUCE

Ingredients:
4 egg yolks
2 tablespoons lemon juice
1/2 pound butter, melted (2 bars)
Salt
Pepper
1/2 cup heavy cream, whipped

Instructions:

Place 4 egg yolks in blender; add 2 tablespoons of lemon juice and blend quickly. Set blender to slow speed and gradually add 1/2 pound of melted butter. Blend for 2 to 3 minutes or until sauce thickens. Salt and pepper to taste. Whip 1/2 cup heavy cream until stiff and fold into sauce.

Thank you very much for your recent letter. I'm delighted that you have given me an opportunity to contribute to the celebration of Will Roger's one hundredth birthday.

As you requested, I'm enclosing one of my family's favorite recipes. I hope that the readership of your cookbook will enjoy Baked Snapper with Crabmeat and Mousseline Sauce as much as we do.

Sincerely,

John D. Rockefeller IV
State of West Virginia

"Had breakfast this morning with John D. Rockefeller, for which I received a fine breakfast and a brand new dime. Went out with him and watched him play eight holes of golf, for which I received another dime.

Made 20 cents clear. Received more jokes from him than I gave, as he is certainly keen and has a great sense of humor.

Had a very pleasant morning and would have stayed longer, but he run out of dimes. I am trying to get him to come to California for his second hundred years.

Who else will give me a dime to eat with them?"

Beef Tenderloin

2 Beef Tenderloin Strips Each Weighing 3-1/2 lbs. Tie Together
Soy Sauce
Worcestershire Sauce
Salt, Garlic Salt
Fresh Ground Pepper
Bacon

Sprinkle beef tenderloin all over with soy sauce and Worcestershire sauce, garlic, regular salt, and fresh ground pepper. On top, crisscross with bacon. Secure with toothpicks. Let stand at room temperature for 3 hours.

Bake the beef tenderloin for 45 minutes at 475 degrees or for 30 minutes at 500 degrees. Let stand 5 minutes, then slice. Serve the beef tenderloin with warm Bearnaise sauce.

BERNAISE SAUCE

1/2 cup dairy sour cream
1/2 cup mayonnaise
2 tablespoons tarragon vinegar
1/2 teaspoon salt
1 teaspoon tarragon leaves
1/2 teaspoon dried shredded green onion

Combine the above ingredients and cover. Refrigerate. Before serving, warm gently. This sauce can be served cold when the tenderloin is served cold.

Serves 10 to 12.

Thanks so much for your recent letter requesting a recipe representative of the State of Kansas. I am more than happy to fulfill this request and I feel compelled to brag a bit on the recipes I am sending.

On February 11, 1975, President Ford visited our capitol city of Topeka and my wife, Olivia, prepared the meal for the President and nine midwestern Governors. All in attendance were very complimentary about the food and Olivia's meal really was a huge success.

Thank you for your interest in the State of Kansas.

Very sincerely,
Robert F. Bennett
Governor of Kansas

Mousse of Sole with Hollandaise

Put in the blender in the following order:
5 files of sole (cut into pieces). Filets must be fresh, not frozen
1 cup light cream
5 eggs
4 egg whites
2 tbsp. melted butter
salt and pepper

Blend mixture for 3 minutes or until smooth. Combine with 1 cup light cream and transfer to a casserole. Put casserole in pan of hot water and bake at 350 degrees for 30 minutes, or until knife inserted in center comes out dry. Serve hot with Hollandaise Sauce. (Serves 6)

Pierre du Pont
Governor, Delaware

Edna Brock's B.B.Q. Beef Brisket

3 lbs. beef brisket
Place one sliced lemon and one medium onion sliced on the brisket. Wrap in heavy foil. Place in a shallow pan. The brisket should fit the pan loosely. Cook in oven six hours at 200 degrees. Cool and slice brisket thinly. Put B.B.Q. sauce on and put in oven two hours more, still wrapped in foil.

B.B.Q. SAUCE

2 c. catsup
2 Tbs. Worcestershire sauce
2 Tsp. prepared mustard
2 Tbs. Liquid smoke
4 Tbs. brown sugar
1/2 Tsp. salt
2 garlic buds crushed (optional)
2 c. water

Donna Raymond
Docent, Will Rogers State Park

"The Stock Market has spoiled more appetites than bad cooking."

Chicken Cacciatora

1/4 cup olive oil
1 teaspoon salt
1 chicken (2-1/2 to 3 lbs., cut up)
2 onions, sliced
1/4 teaspoon pepper
2 cloves garlic, minced
1 can (1 lb.) Italian tomatoes
1 8 oz. can tomato sauce
1/2 teaspoon celery seed
1 teaspoon crushed, dried oregano
2 bay leaves
1/2 cup dry white wine

Heat oil in large deep skillet. Brown chicken in it. Remove chicken and keep hot. Cook onions and garlic in oil in skillet until tender. Add other ingredients, except wine, and blend. Cook 5 minutes. Return chicken to skillet. Cover and simmer 45 minutes. Add wine, and cook uncovered about 15 minutes or until chicken is tender. Arrange on hot platter. Skim any excess fat from sauce and remove bay leaves. Pour sauce over chicken and serve with spaghetti or noodles.

Serves 4 to 6.

Governor Thomas Judge

State of Montana

Rouladen

1 Slice Round Steak – 1/4″ thick (ask butcher to pound it)
Bacon
Onion
Salt
Mustard
Flour
Pepper

Trim out the bone and trim off all fat. Fry fat in skillet or electric skillet. Cut meat along veins, a few will be large, cut these in half.

Spread each piece with mustard, then a strip of bacon and some chopped onion. Roll into bundles and secure with 2 round toothpicks.

Dredge in flour and brown in fat already prepared. Usually it will be necessary to add some shortening.

A good brown crust adds to the flavor of this dish, so do not hurry this process. When all are browned, add water and cover pan. Simmer or bake for 1-1/2 or 2 hours, adding water as necessary.

I am sending you the recipe for Rouladen, and I hope you find it as delectable as I do. Best wishes and good luck on your cookbook to be used in the celebration of the birthday anniversary of Will Rogers.

Kindest personal regards,

Otis R. Bowen, M.D.
Governor
State of Indiana

Veal Parmigiana a la New Mexico

1 lb. thinly sliced veal cutlets (about 6)
1 egg, slightly beaten
3/4 cup fine dry seasoned bread crumbs
1/4 cup butter or margarine
1 16 oz. jar meatless spaghetti sauce
8 oz. mozzarella cheese, sliced
1 4 oz. can chopped green chili (more if desired)
1 4 oz. can mushrooms, drained
Grated Parmesan cheese

Preheat oven to 350 degrees.

Dip veal cutlets first in egg and then coat well with bread crumbs. Heat butter in skillet over moderately low heat; add veal and increase temperature to moderately high and brown veal well on both sides. Pour a layer of spaghetti sauce into bottom of a shallow 2-qt. baking dish. Arrange veal in a single layer over sauce. Spread green chili evenly over veal; then arrange sliced mozzarella over chili. Add drained mushrooms to remaining sauce and pour over cheese.

Sprinkle generously with Parmesan cheese and bake 35 minutes.

Serve with additional grated Parmesan cheese if desired. Serves 4.

I am enclosing a recipe for Veal Parmigiana a la New Mexico, which is a favorite of the Apodaca family. I hope your readers will enjoy it.

My best wishes for the success of this very worthwhile project.

Sincerely,

Jerry Apodaca
Governor, New Mexico

43

Chili and Beans

Grind 1 pound of round steak and one onion, salt to taste and saute until brown. Then add one can of tomatoes, one small can of pimento (or take two fresh pimentos and skin, putting in hot oven or over gas jet until skins will come off easily) and chop fine. Cook this one hour. Then add two cans of red kidney beans, or soak two cups of red kidney beans overnight and cook over very slow fire.

Will Rogers

This recipe was first published in the Beverly Hills Woman's club cookbook in 1931. We thank the club for permission to reprint it.

Baked Ham

Use Swift's Premium. Score fat. Rub in all the brown sugar you can and stud with cloves. Make a paste of 8 cups of flour and water. Roll out and wrap ham. Save a piece of the dough to patch with as the steam will force holes through the dough. Put ham in roaster and add a little boiling water to keep from burning. Roast 5 or 6 hours, more if necessary depending on the size of ham. Break off dough; put ham in oven to brown. A little sweet pickle juice is good poured over ham before putting in oven to brown.

Will Rogers

Printed in the Beverly Hills Women's Cookbook–1931

"When you get a group of women behind anything it is always a success."

Egg Timbales with Cheese Sauce

3 eggs
6 tablespoons whole milk
salt and pepper to taste

Beat eggs slightly, add milk, seasonings, and beat again. Butter timbale molds or custard cups, and fill two-thirds full. Place in pan of hot water and bake in 325 degree oven until firm about 25 minutes.

SAUCE
1 tablespoon flour
1 tablespoon butter
2/3 cup milk (or beer)
3/4 Ib. New York State sharp cheddar cheese, grated.

Melt butter, stir in flour until smooth, gradually add milk (or beer), add grated cheese and stir until smooth.

Turn out molds on serving platter and pour sauce over. Garnish with sauteed bacon and chopped parsley. Serve very hot.

Governor Hugh Carey
State of New York

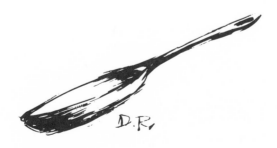

Baked Pork Chops

Oven - 350°

Ingredients:
pork chops - one per person
cooked white rice - about 1/3 C. per chop
frozen corn - about 1 10 oz. pkg. per 6 chops
onion - one slice per chop
tomato - one slice per chop
bell pepper - one slice per chop
salt and pepper

Preparation:
Lightly spray bottom of baking dish with Pam. Use a baking dish just large enough to fit the number of pork chops you are using in a single layer on the bottom. Place uncooked chops in baking dish and lightly season with salt and pepper. Spoon rice atop each chop and layer rest of ingredients in the order given. Cover dish with foil. Place in preheated oven and bake for one hour. Serve one per plate. Add a salad and bread.

You can assemble this in the morning and it's ready to go into the oven when it's dinnertime. It's an easy company dish when time is short.

Carol Sandmeier
Volunteer, William S. Hart Ranch

"No man is great if he thinks he is."

Ham Loaf

1 lb. cured ham, chopped
1/2 lb. fresh ham, chopped
1-1/2 c. dry bread crumbs
2 eggs
3/4 c. milk
Pepper

Dressing:
1/2 c. water
1/4 c. sugar
1/4 c. vinegar
1 Tbs. mustard

Mix first group of ingredients well, form into loaf shape. Pour dressing over loaf, bake 1-1/2 hours at 350 degrees. Baste frequently. Serves 6.

Lt. Col. John H. Glenn, Jr.
U. S. M. C.
America's first orbital astronaut
February 20, 1962
John Glenn is also a U. S. Senator
from Ohio

"I like to make little jokes and kid about the Senators. They are a never-ending source of amusement, amazement and discouragement. But the rascals, when you meet 'em they are mighty nice fellows. It must be something in the office that makes 'em so honery sometimes. When you see what they do officially, you want to shoot 'em, but when one looks at you and grins so innocently, you kinder want to kiss him."

Wild Onions and Eggs

2 c. onions
6 Tbsp. bacon grease
1 c. water
6 beaten eggs

Clean and wash enough onions to make two cups, cut in one inch lengths. Put in a skillet with water, cook until tender. Pour off excess water. Season with bacon grease; cook five minutes. Add beaten eggs, stir until eggs are cooked. Add salt and pepper to taste. Serves 4.

Gazella Lane

Member of the Pocahontas Woman's Club of Claremore, Oklahoma

"We will never have true civilization until we have learned to recognize the rights of others."

"Chili Pie"

7 oz. can green roasted chilis
1 dozen eggs–well beaten
3/4 lb. grated cheese (sharp yellow cheese)
2 cans cream corn (optional)

Line baking dish, 3 to 4 qt. capacity, with green chilis, add cheese and well beaten eggs. Bake at 375 degrees 30-40 minutes.

If you want a more souffle type dish you can separate 1/2 the eggs beat separately and fold in.

Patricia Z. Stephenson

Mrs. Stephenson is the daughter of Flo Ziegfeld and Billie Burke. The Ziegfelds were friends of the Rogers family, and of course Will Rogers worked in the "Ziegfeld Follies".

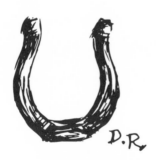

During World War I, Will Rogers was delivering his monologue in the Ziegfeld Follies one evening when a hatchet-faced woman in the ninth row called out, "Why aren't you in the Army?" Rogers gave everybody in the audience time to turn around and look at his heckler, then drawled, "For the same reason, madam, that you aren't in the Follies: physical disabilities."

Sarma

1 cup rice
1-1/2 pound ground pork
1 pound ground ham
1/2 pound ground beef
1 large onion
1/8 tsp. minced garlic
1 egg
1 large head soured cabbage
2 quarts sauerkraut
salt and pepper
strips of bacon

Place cabbage in large pan of water, core head and separate leaves. Wash each leaf and drain in colander. Wash sauerkraut and drain. Dice onion and brown lightly in fat, mix with meat, garlic, rice, seasonings and egg. Roll a generous portion of meat mixture in each leaf. When leaves are gone, shape rest of meat into balls. Cover bottom of large roaster pan with kraut and place rolls on top. If it is necessary to have more than one layer of rolls, place a layer of kraut between. End with a layer of kraut on top and place strips of bacon over kraut. Nearly cover with cold water. Bake covered at 350 degrees for about two hours. Approximately 22 Sarmas from 3 pounds of meat.

You will find enclosed a recipe for sarma, which represents Governor and Mrs. Perpich's ethnic background. The sarma is a Croatian main dish. It is a favorite of the Governor and his family.

Governor and Mrs. Rudy Perpich
of Minnesota

Stuffed Mushrooms Italiano

1 pound fresh mushrooms
1 stalk celery, chopped
1 small onion, minced
1 small clove garlic, crushed
1/4 cup Italian style bread crumbs
1/4 cup parmesan cheese
1 small egg, beaten
white wine, optional
salt and pepper

Wash mushrooms, break off stems and chop.

Arrange whole mushroom caps on baking sheet (for added flavor, sprinkle caps with white wine).

Bake in preheated oven (350 degrees) about 5 minutes while preparing filling.

Saute chopped stems, celery, onion and garlic in butter until onion is transparent, about 5 minutes.

Allow mushroom caps and saute to cool slightly.

Add bread crumbs, cheese, egg and salt and pepper to saute.

Stuff mushroom caps and return to 350 degree oven for 10 minutes. Serve hot.

I am pleased to enclose a recipe for Stuffed Mushrooms Italiano which is a family favorite.

With best wishes,   Cordially,

                                     Ella Grasso

                                     Ella Grasso
                                     Governor
                                     State of Connecticut

51

Chicken Almond

Boil four chicken breasts, in ample water until tender. Add 2 bay leaves, 1 large onion, and 1 cup celery tops. Cook all at once. Retain broth. Cool chicken and cut in bite-size pieces.

Fry 2 lbs. sausage. Pour off fat. In small amount of the fat, fry one large bunch celery (about one cup), one bell pepper, two large onions, cut fine. Simmer until nearly tender.

In a large casserole pour 9 cups liquid (water and broth from cooking chicken), 2 cups rice (brown or white), one cup wild rice. 3 pkg. Lipton chicken noodle soup, 1 cup blanched almonds, 2 cans sliced mushrooms. Add all other ingredients. Cook covered, in 375 degree oven, 1-1/2 hours. Take cover off the last 10 minutes. Cover with slivered almonds. Stir twice while cooking.

Donna Raymond
Docent, Will Rogers State Park

Western Barbequed Burgers

One pound ground beef
1/2 medium onion. chopped
3 tbls. Worchestershire Sauce
3 tbls. barbeque sauce (your favorite)
Add to taste: garlic salt, black pepper, and chili powder

Mix all of the above together and make into four hamburger patties.
Cook on barbeque and serve on onion or kaiser rolls.
Serves 4.

Kathy Holt
Park Maintenance Worker 1

"You have to have a serious streak in you or you can't see the funny side of the other fellow."

Quick Swedish Meatballs

Ground chopped beef in quantities to suit size of your group.

Add bread crumbs and seasoning to taste.

Roll very lightly into tiny meatballs and saute, preferably in their own fat, at least to start.

At the same time, open a can of cranberry sauce (either jellied or whole) and a can or jar of ready made spaghetti sauce (your favorite brand).

Blend together well, add meatballs, simmer, and serve on a bed of instant rice.

Milton J. Sharp
State of Pennsylvania

"If we can just improve their (women's) marksmanship, we can improve civilization. About every fourth fellow you meet nowadays ought to be shot."

"California Chili"

3 lbs. Round Steak (cut 1/2 inch cubes-trim fat)
2 onions chopped
12 cloves garlic (finely chopped)
6 Tbs. olive oil
1 6 oz. can tomato paste
4 Tbs. Chili Powder
1 Tbs. Cumin
1-1/2 Tbs. paprika – 1 Tbs. oregano – 2 Tbs. salt – 1 Tbs. red pepper flakes
1/2 bell pepper
2 bay leaves
4 grindings black pepper corns
4 cup beef broth
5 cans small red beans

Heat 4 Tbsp. olive oil, in a large iron pot, add meat. Stir constantly till lightly browned. Remove meat to a large casserole. Add remainder oil to iron pot. Cook onion and garlic in oil about 4 min. Remove pot from heat. Add all other ingredients. Remove bay leaves after 20 minutes. Let simmer at least two hours.

Serve with a green salad and garlic-cheese bread.

Hal Roach

"You can always judge a town by the quality of the chili."

(B and O) Railroad Stew

1-1/2 lbs. stewing beef – sear (brown)
salt and pepper
1 large onion, diced – sear
Add one large can of solid packed tomatoes
Stew on low heat – add a bit of flour and water to thicken like gravy
Last 10 minutes, add one package of frozen peas
Serve on a bed of mashed potatoes
Serves 4-5.

If Will Rogers ever rode the train in his vaudeville days, he may have eaten this railroad stew. More than 50 years ago, my great uncle served this stew on the B and O Railroad. I believe it would not spill out of the dish if the train came to an emergency halt.

My grandmother doubled this recipe to serve her ten children.

Ethel Haydon
Docent, Will Rogers State Park

"We can't go through life just eating cake all the time."

Mrs. Rogers' Southern Green Beans

2 lbs. string beans
1/2 lb. salt pork
1 medium onion, peeled
1 quart water
Salt and pepper

Cut beans approximately 1-1/2 inches in length. Cube and brown salt pork. Bring water to boil, add beans, salt pork, onion and salt and pepper to taste. Simmer slowly 2 to 3 hours.

Submitted by Mr. Emil Sandmeier who worked for the Rogers family for many years and reports that very simple dishes were served at the Ranch House.

"Of course, the Mother I know the most about is the Mother of our little group. She has been for 22 years trying to raise to maturity, four children, three by birth and one by marriage. While she hasent done a good job, the poor soul has done all that mortal human could do with the material she has had to work with."

Will Rogers "Good Old Oklahoma Beans"

2 lbs. small white navy beans
1 generous ham hock
1 medium onion, peeled
Salt and pepper

Soak beans over night in cold water. In the morning, drain and cover with fresh water. Bring to boil, add ham hock, onion, salt and pepper to taste. Simmer slowly for 4 hours. Add more water, if necessary so beans will be kind of soupy. Each serving should include a partion of ham.

Emil Sandmeier

Docent, Will Rogers State Park

"Left New York at 1 P.M. today; am at Cleveland at 5 P.M., and will be in Beverly tomorrow night for corn bread and beans."

Lasagne

1 lb. ground beef
1 clove garlic, minced
2 tblsp. salad oil
1 can (1 lb. 4 oz.) solid pack tomatoes
1 can (8 oz.) tomato sauce
1 tsp. salt
1/2 tsp. pepper
1/2 tsp. oregano
1/2 lb. Lasagne noodles, cooked just tender
1 lb. ricotta or dry cottage cheese
1/2 cup grated Parmesan cheese
1/2 lb. Mozzarella cheese, sliced

Brown beef and garlic in oil, stirring with a fork. Add tomatoes, first draining off half the juice; add tomato sauce and seasonings. Simmer for 30 min. Cook noodles, drain and rinse. Cover bottom of a large greased baking dish with 1-1/2 cups of beef mixture. Cover the beef mixture with a single layer of noodles. Spread 1/2 of the ricotta cheese on the noodles, sprinkle with 1/2 the Parmesan cheese and place over this 1/3 of the Mozzarella cheese. Repeat. Top with remaining beef mixture and mozzarella. Bake in 350° oven for 45 min. Let stand 15 min. after removing from oven. Cut into squares.

Willard Cruse
Will Rogers Park groundskeeper and
horticulturist since 1953

"Wherever you find poor soil, you will always find politics."

Baked Chicken Hollandaise

2 - (2-1/2 lb) Broiling chickens, cut in serving pieces
1/2 cup flour
1 tsp. salt
1/2 tsp. onion salt
1 tsp. dried tarragon (optional)
1/2 Clove garlic, slivered
1/4 Cup *each* oil and margarine
1/2 Cup mayonnaise
2 tsp. lemon juice
1/2 tsp. dry mustard
1/2 cup crushed crisp cereal flakes

Dust chicken pieces with a mixture of flour, salt, onion salt and tarragon. Fry the garlic in oil and margarine in a large skillet for a few seconds, then add the chicken. Brown a few pieces at a time until both sides are evenly colored – about 15 minutes. Arrange in one layer in a greased bake dish, skin side down, and add 3 tablespoons water. Cover and bake at 350 degrees for 30 minutes. Uncover and turn chicken over. Spread with a mixture of the mayonnaise, lemon juice and mustard. Sprinkle with a coating of the crisp cereal flakes and bake uncovered at 375 degrees for 20 minutes, or until top is bubbly brown and chicken very tender. Sprinkle with paprika.

Serves 8.

Frances and Bryan Sterling
Authors

"Shakespeare is the only author that can play to losing business for a hundred years and still be known as an author."

Baked Stuffed Shrimp

Buy frozen jumbo shrimp (allow 4 to a serving). Thaw them; drain them. Flatten shrimp in a buttered shallow baking pan. Top with following dressing:

1 cup rolled cracker crumbs
1 cup finely crushed potato chips
1 stick butter or margarine melted
1 pint scallops, put through food grinder, raw

Season with garlic salt, onion salt, just a dash celery salt.

Enough milk to make light and fluffy dressing.

Put generous amount of dressing on each flattened-out shrimp. This is enough for 16 to 20 jumbo shrimp. Sprinkle generously with grated Parmesan cheese. Bake at 350 degrees about 20 minutes or until shrimp meat has turned white.

James B. Longley

Governor

State of Maine

Beef Teriyaki

2 lbs. sirloin tip or 4-5 steaks
2/3 C soy sauce
1/2 C sugar
1 t. monosodium glutamate
2 T. green onions, chopped
1 t. fresh ginger root, grated
5 cloves garlic, chopped
1 T. sesame oil (optional)
1 T. sesame seeds, crushed (optional)

Combine all ingredients except beef. Additional sugar may be added to sweeten.

Marinate beef a half hour before grilling.

Governor George R. Ariyoshi
State of Hawaii

"Hawaii is the only place I know where they lay flowers on you while you are alive."

Layered Tortilla Pie

1 pound ground beef
1 medium onion, chopped
1 clove garlic, minced
1 tablespoon butter or margarine
1 (8-ounce) can tomato sauce
1 (2-1/4 ounce) can sliced ripe olives, drained
1 tablespoon chili powder
1 teaspoon salt
1/4 teaspoon pepper
6 corn tortillas, buttered
2 cups shredded longhorn Cheddar cheese
1/2 cup water

Brown beef, onion and garlic in butter. Drain. Add tomato sauce, olives, chili powder, salt and pepper. In a round 2-quart casserole, alternate layers of tortillas, meat sauce and 1-1/2 cups cheese. Sprinkle remaining 1/2 cup cheese over top. Pour water at edge of casserole into bottom. Cover and bake at 400 degrees 25 minutes. Uncover and let stand 5 minutes before cutting in wedges. Makes 4 servings.

Ruth Bloch
Docent, Will Rogers State Park

"Happiness and contentment is progress. In fact that's all progress is."

Stuffed Ham Seville

1 can mandarin oranges
1/4 Cup orange marmalade
1/4 teaspoon ground ginger
3 Cups cooked rice
1/4 Cup chopped pecans (optional)
3 tablespoons sliced onion
1/4 Cup mayonnaise or salad dressing
6 large thin slices of baked ham.

(1) Drain liquid from mandarin oranges. Cook liquid rapidly until reduced by half; then stir in marmalade and ginger.

(2) Set aside 12 mandarin orange segments. Mix with remaining other ingredients (except ham) in a bowl. Spoon about 3/4 Cup onto each slice of ham. Fold ham over to cover filling and place in a shallow baking dish. Brush with part of hot orange sauce.

(3) Bake in a moderate 350 degree oven, brushing with remaining orange sauce for about 25 minutes. Garnish with saved mandarin orange segments. Bake 5 minutes longer.

Governor David L. Boren
State of Oklahoma

Will was born in Oklahoma on November 4, 1879.

"Politicians can do more funny things naturally than I can think of to do purposely."

64

Lobster Ragout

1 lb. lobster meat (canned chunk)
1 can condensed cream of chicken soup
3/4 cup light cream
1 can chicken gumbo soup – condensed
1/2 tsp. Worcestershire sauce
1 tsp. curry powder
1/2 cup dry sherry wine

1. Put lobster meat, both soups, light cream, worcestershire sauce, curry powder and sherry into top of double boiler on chafing dish over water. Mix thoroughly . . . but gently . . . so as not to break lobster chunks.

2. Cook gently until the curry is cooked and hot. (It is best to blend curry powder with a little butter or warm water for easier blending.)

3. Serve on hot plates over toast points. Serves four (4).

If you do not use toast points . . . do serve crisp French bread. A green salad goes well. Crab meat may be substituted for lobster.

I have enclosed Mrs. Byrne's recipe for LOBSTER RAGOUT which has been a favorite of the family for many years.

Sincerely,

Brendan T. Byrne
Govenor, State of New Jersey

Chicken Enchiladas Babbitt

4 Chicken Breasts (or 1 whole chicken) cooked, deboned & cubed
12 Corn Tortillas
1 8 oz. can chopped Green Chilis
1 can Cream of Chicken soup
1 can Cream of Mushroom soup
(add 1/2 t. ground Coriander to soups and heat)
1 large onion, diced
1/2 lb. Cheddar cheese, grated
1/2 lb. Monterey Jack cheese, grated

Line 2-3 qt. casserole with Tortillas after dipping in warm oil. Layer cubed chicken, green chili, diced onion, undiluted soups mixtures, then cheese. Repeat layering until ingredients are used, topping off with cheese. Bake in 350 degree oven approximately 1 hour.

(Individual enchilladas may be made by filling one corn tortilla with the ingredients, lay side-by-side in shallow baking pan, cover with soup mix and grated cheese and bake 20-30 mins.) Top with chopped green onions before serving if you like things spicy!

Raul Castro
Governor — State of Arizona

"The best way to judge just how good a man is, is to find out how he stands around his home and among his kind of people."

Julian's Chili

2 lbs. ground beef
1 medium onion
1 pkg. spaghetti
2 cans chili beans
3/4 cup sugar
2 cans tomato paste
1 qt. home-canned tomato juice
4 to 6 tsp. chili powder
1/2 cup red wine
Salt and garlic to taste

Brown ground beef and onions together. Cook spaghetti in three quarts salt water: Retain water for part of liquid. Add other ingredients. Simmer for 1-1/2 hours. Add red wine 30 minutes before done.

Note: Except for the addition of the wine, which is Charlann's suggestion, this is the recipe Governor Carroll used when he cooked for his brothers and sisters as a boy.

A favorite recipe of

Governor & Mrs. Julian M. Carroll of Kentucky

Governor Ray's All time Favorite Bouillabaisse

3 cans (1 pound 4 ounces each) stewed tomatoes
2 large onions, chopped
4 cups celery, chopped into 1-inch strips
1 green pepper, chopped
Juice of 2 oranges and 1 Tbsp grated orange rind
1 small can (about 3 oz.) chicken soup base
Salt and pepper to taste
Assorted seasonings (1/2 tsp. each garlic, tarragon, dill weed or dill seed) tied into cheesecloth bag
1 Tbsp. parsley
1 cup of your favorite red wine (dry)
2 to 4 pounds fresh salmon, cut into chunks
2 to 4 pounds fresh halibut or other white fish, cut into chunks
1 to 2 pounds each raw scallops, frozen shrimp, whole well-scrubbed clams and any other raw seafood
Legs, claws and body chunks of fresh crab

Into large heavy soup kettle mix tomatoes, onions, celery, green pepper, juice and rind of oranges, salt, pepper, parsley and assorted seasonings in cheesecloth bag. Cover kettle and bring to a slow boil. Continue to simmer for one hour. Add red wine.

20 minutes before serving add all the fish and seafood EXCEPT CRAB.
5 minutes before serving add the crab.

Be sure Bouillabaisse is kept at full simmer until serving. Serve in large soup bowls accompanied by hot garlic french bread.

Large napkins or small tea towels are a necessity. Be prepared for 2 to 3 servings per person.

Recipe serves 8 to 12.

This is a fun recipe . . . Keep tasting and testin . . . Add your own favorite seasonings. Important . . . ! . . . do not simmer away too much of the soup . . . it may be very necessary to add more liquid . . . use water or tomato juice.

I am happy to enclose my favorite bouillabaisse recipe for the Will Rogers cookbook. I am grateful for your invitation to visit his California ranch house.

Sincerely,

Dixy Lee Ray
Governor
State of Washington

Hungarian Goulash with Noodles

Serves 25
5 Lbs. Beef Rump or Round, cubed
1 Qt. Onion, finely chopped
1 Clove Garlic, finely chopped

Brown the meat, onion and garlic in suet or vegetable oil.

Add:
1-1/2 Teaspoon dry mustard
1/4 Cup Paprika
1/2 Cup and 1 Tablespoon Brown Sugar
1 Tablespoon salt
1 Cup Worcestershire Sauce
1 Tablespoon Vinegar
2 Cups Catsup
1 Qt. Water
1 Qt. Beef Consomme

Mix, cook, add to meat and simmer until tender.

Strain meat and thicken juice with 2 cups plus 1 tablespoon flour, mixed with cold water. Return meat to gravy.

Cook *wide* noodles until slightly underdone. Then divide into baking pans and mix with the meat mixture.

Reheat pans about 1/2 hour before serving to guests. If they stand long, mix with a bit of water and reheat.

This is one of our family favorites and is highly representative of the State of North Dakota since we are a leading producer of beef.

I would be happy to have the opportunity sometime to visit Will Rogers ranch home. I'm sure that would be a very intersting tour.

Sincerely,

Arthur A. Link
Governor
North Dakota

Rice Dressing

2 pounds lean ground beef
1 cup chopped white onions
1 cup chopped celery
1 cup chopped sweet green peppers
Dry mustard, salt, pepper and cayenne pepper to taste
1 cup short-grain rice

Saute ground meat in large, heavy saucepan (black cast iron, preferably) until browned well. Add half of the chopped ingredients and seasonings. Continue to cook over low fire for about one hour, keeping moist by adding small amounts of water as needed.

In the meantime, cook rice – 1 cup of rice/two cups of water.

After meat mixture has simmered one hour, add remaining chopped ingredients and continue to cook approximately 45 minutes, adding again, small amounts of water as needed.

When ready to serve, combine rice with meat mixture and serve at once.

Thank you very much for advising me of the cookbook the Docent Organization is preparing in commemoration of Will Rogers 100th Birthday. I am pleased to enclose my favorite recipe to be used in this cookbook and I am honored by your request.

Best wishes.

Cordially

Edwin Edwards
State of Louisiana

71

Seafood a la Newberg

2 cups Hot medium white sauce
2 egg yolks, beaten
3 cups seafood (shrimp, crab, lobster)
Mix together carefully, serve hot over toast points in patty shells.
Garnish with parsley and lemon

Medium White Sauce
3 Tbls. butter
3 Tbls. flour
1/2 tsp.salt
Pepper to taste
1 cup milk

Melt butter in a heavy saucepan, low heat. Use a wooden spoon for stirring. Blend in flour, cook over low heat, stirring until mixture is smooth and bubbly. Remove from heat, stir in milk, salt, and pepper, Return to stove, bring to boil, reduce heat and cook until mixture thickens, stirring constantly, about ten minutes. Fold in seafood.

Juliet Schoen-Managing Editor
Palisadian Post

"A breakfast without a newspaper is like a horse without a saddle, you are just riding bareback."

Franks and Peppers

(Ciabotta, from the Italian Ciabottare, which means to shuffle)

6 Franks
6 Sweet frying peppers
2 Hot Italian peppers
28 oz. can crushed tomatoes
3 Eggs
3 T. Olive oil
Salt

Cut franks into 1/4 inch slices. Core and seed peppers and cut into quarters or smaller. Saute together in the olive oil in a heavy skillet until peppers are almost soft. Add tomatoes, bring to a boil and cook uncovered for 10 minutes. Crack eggs into mixture and stir with a fork until eggs are cooked. Salt to taste. Serve with lots of Italian bread for dunking. (For those brave of heart increase proportion of hot peppers). Serves 4 to 6.

Dick Latessa

Clem Rogers in
The Will Rogers Follies

P.S. My Mom always made this for us when she was between washing and ironing and in a rush to get to work. It's easy and quick to make, and in those days would feed the seven of us for about a dollar.

"My Daddy fought with (General) Stand Watie in the Confederacy, but you couldent get much war news out of Papa. I sho dident inherit this continuous flow of blathering around from him."

Quick Quiche

1/2 cup margarine
1/2 cup flour
1 pint cottage cheese
1 4oz. can chopped green chilis (undrained)
10 eggs
1 tsp. baking powder
1 lb. Monterey Jack cheese, grated
1/2 tsp. salt

Melt margarine in 9x13 pan. Beat eggs in bowl, lightly. Add flour and baking powder, blend. Add all remaining ingredients including the melted butter from the pan. Blend well, pour in pan, bake at 400° for 15 minutes. Reduce oven to 350°, continue baking for 35 minutes.

This is good served hot as an Hors d'oeuvre - just cut in small squares and have picks for spearing.

Alice Karl
Docent, Will Rogers State Park

Marie Spota's Lemon Chicken or Fish

6 pieces of chicken or fish (or one piece for each serving)
2 eggs, beaten
1 cup corn flake crumbs
garlic crushed
2 Tbls. Flour
1/2 cup white chablis
1/2 cup chicken broth
1/2 cup juice from a fresh lemon

Dip meat or fish in the beaten egg, roll in corn flake crumbs, fry in hot olive oil seasoned with lemon herb (McCormic) salt and fresh garlic minced on both sides as you fry.

Place chicken or fish in a serving dish as you fry it. In fry pan drippings saute 1 tbls. fresh garlic, minced. Make a roux of 2 tbls. flour and 2 tbls. olive oil, start adding 1/2 cup white Chablis, 1/2 cup chicken broth and the 1/2 cup fresh lemon juice. Boil until a thick gravy forms, pour over meat. Serve immediately.

George and Maria Spoda
Will Rogers U.S.A.

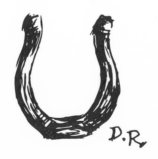

Wild Rice Hot Dish

1 cup wild rice
3 medium chopped onions
1 diced green pepper
1 pound ground beef

Brown onions, pepper and beef in 2 tablespoons butter. Do not season.
1 can cream of mushroom soup
1 can mushrooms and juice
3 to 4 ounces soy sauce
1 small can sliced water chestnuts
3 cups water

Add soup, mushrooms, soy sauce, chestnuts and water to ground beef mixture and mix thoroughly.

Drain wild rice and mix with other ingredients. Place in casserole. 1/8 cup cashews may be sprinkled on top if desired. Bake 1-1/2 hours at 350 degrees. Makes 6 average servings.

Walter F. Mondale

Walter Mondale
Vice President of
the United States

Roast Pheasant

1 or 2 pheasant
1 stick butter
1/2 onion, chopped
flour, salt and pepper
1/2 cup Crisco
1 can mushroom soup

Cut up bird(s) - cut breast off bone and separate into four (4) steaks. If birds are in good supply it is nicer to use just the breast and legs. Dredge pieces in seasoned flour; brown in mixture of butter and Crisco. Place browned pieces in roasting pan. Cook onions in same pan until limp and golden, adding more butter or Crisco if needed. Add mushroom soup to onions, mix well and pour over pheasant in roaster. Rinse onion pan with a little water and add. Cover roaster, cook in 325 degree oven about 2 hours. Watch the last half hour so the birds don't dry too much.

Optional:
Add 1 clove garlic minced, 1/4 tsp. rosemary, 1/4 tsp. parsley, 1/4 cup white wine and 1/2 cup water to pan with onions and cook 5 minutes, then add mushroom soup and finish recipe. Omit rinsing the pan with water if this method is used.

Alice Karl
Docent Will Rogers State Park

"It will take America fifteen years steady taking care of our own business and letting everybody else's alone to get us back to where everybody speaks to us again."

Joe's Fried Chicken

1 Chicken (clean and cut into pieces)
Mix:
2 to 3 cups milk
2 unbeaten eggs
Soak cleaned chicken in milk and egg mixture for one-half hour.

Remove chicken, season with salt and pepper, sprinkle with paprika, roll in mixture of two parts crushed corn flakes and one part flour. Deep fry in pure vegetable oil.

If you wish, you may mix the salt, pepper, paprika, crushed corn flakes and flour together, and roll chicken in mixture.

Governor Joseph P. Teasdale
State of Missouri

"That's what makes us a great country. The little things are serious and the big ones are not."

Sauerbraten Al a Elizabeth

Soak 4 pound chuck roast in:
2-1/2 cups vinegar
2 cups water
1/2 cup ketchup
1 large onion, sliced
1/4 cup brown sugar
3/4 tsp. ground cloves
salt and pepper to taste

Refrigerate and soak meat at least one week in above, turning daily.

Heat and bring to a boil, reduce temperature and simmer covered (Till bubbly) 1-2 hours (Do not add any additional vinegar or water while cooking) when meat is tender, take out and make gravy. Slice meat and return to gravy. Heat.

Serve over cooked noodles.

> Gregory Malak-Curator
> Will Rogers Memorial
> Claremore, Oklahoma

"People are marvelous in their generosity if they just know the cause is there."

Seasoning for Venison Steaks, Fish, Chicken and Beef

2 tsp. onion salt
1/4 tsp. seasoned pepper
1 Tbsp. dried chives
1 Tbsp. chervil
2 tsp. seasoned salt
1 Tbsp. parsley
1 Tbsp. marjoram leaves
1 Tbsp. tarragon leaves
2 envelopes instant chicken broth or 1 jar instant chicken broth

Place all ingredients in blender, mix until there is a fine powder. Store in tightly covered jar. When ready to use mix 4 tsp. of seasoning with 1 cup of flour, dredge steaks in flour mixture. Brown steaks in hot shortening. This mixture may be used with fish, chicken and beef too.

Alice Karl
Docent, Will Rogers State Park

"There is still a lot of monkey in us. Throw anything you want in our cage and we will give it serious consideration."

Barbequed Tequila-Lime Fajitas

1/2 cup lime juice
1/4 cup tequila
1/4 cup cooking oil
1 4-ounce can chopped chili peppers, drained
1/2 teaspoon bottled hot pepper sauce
1/4 teaspoon salt
1 medium onion, thinly sliced
1 boneless beef plate skirt steak or flank steak about 3/4 pound
6 8-inch flour or corn tortillas
1 large can refried beans

For marinade, in 2-cup measure, combine lime juice tequila, oil, chili peppers, hot pepper sauce and salt. Add onion. Place steak in a shallow dish. Pour marinade over steak. Cover and marinate steak in the refrigerator overnight, turning several times.

Remove steak from marinade reserving the marinade, pat steak dry with towel. Remove onion and chili peppers from marinade, wrap all in foil. Stack tortillas and chili and wrap in another piece of foil.

Grill the wrapped onions and chili peppers and the steak directly over medium coals for about 10 minutes, then add the wrapped tortillas and heat for another ten minutes or so. Baste steak with marinade reserve.

To serve, slice steak thinly, place steak, onions, chili peppers, refried beans, lettuce, olives and any other fillers onto serving platters. Line these up with tortillas and serve, build your own. This makes about three servings.

David A. Matthews
State Park Ranger 1

81

Mike Cramers
Hungarian Beef Paprikash

3/4 lb. beef sirloin
2 cups beef stock (broth)
2 T. canola oil
2 T. paprika
1/2 chopped onion
1/2 cup sliced button mushrooms
1 clove garlic, minced
salt and black pepper
1-1/2 T. butter (or margarine)
1 T. flour
1/2 cup sour cream
2 teaspoons lemon juice
cooked egg noodles

Slice beef into thin strips. Heat in 1 T. of canola oil (in stockpot) and saute until cooked through. Remove beef with slotted spoon and set aside. Pour off excess oil. Heat 1 T. canola oil and butter in same pot and add onion and garlic. Saute until tender (*not* brown) Now add cooked beef, beef stock, mushrooms and paprika. Bring to a boil then reduce heat and cover and simmer on low heat for 1 hour.

Mix flour and sour cream together Add to stock pot. Turn up heat and continue stirring until thickened. Stir in lemon juice. Remove from heat, keep covered for 5 minutes. Add salt and pepper to taste. Serve over freshly cooked egg noodles. Serves 2-4 adults.

Mikal Sandoval Cramer
State Park Ranger 1

Chicken Supreme

6 chicken breast pieces (skinless and boneless)
1 can cream of chicken soup
8 oz. sour cream
1/4 c white wine
1/4 tsp. dill
1/4 tsp. curry
1 tbs. dried onion
1/4 tsp. garlic powder
1/4 tsp. lemon pepper
4-6 oz. fresh mushrooms, sliced
1 small can sliced water chestnuts
3 c cooked white rice

Saute chicken pieces in butter until brown, but not cooked. Set aside. Mix remaining ingredients for sauce. Place rice in 8x8 flat casserole. Cut chicken into serving size pieces and place on top of rice. Pour sauce over all. Bake 375° 50-60 minutes until bubbly. (If preferred, you can use chicken thighs.)

Serves 8.

Eleanor Nichols
Docent, Will Rogers State Park

Veal Scaloppine

1 clove garlic, quartered
2 Tbs. vegetable oil
4 veal cutlets
1 Tbs. flour
pepper to taste
1/4 tsp. ground nutmeg
1 small onion-thinly sliced
1/2 cup Marsale wine
1/2 pound mushrooms, sliced
1/2 tsp. paprika
2 Tbs. chopped parsely

Saute garlic in oil over low heat 5 min. Discard garlic. Brown cutlets on both sides, in garlic seasoned oil. Combine flour, pepper, and nutmeg, sprinkle over browned meat, add onion and wine, simmer 20 minutes. Turn meat occasionally, add more wine if needed. Add mushrooms to pan and cook covered ten minutes. Serve on a warm platter with sauce. Garnish with paprika and parsley. Makes 4 serving

Marjorie Hanson
Docent, Will Rogers State Park

Tijuana Hamburger Torte

1 lb. ground beef
1 can stewed tomatoes
1 can chopped green chilies
12 corn tortillas
1 med. onion, chopped
1 can tomato sauce
1 package taco season mix
1 lb. cheddar cheese, grated

Brown beef, onions in skillet. Add stewed tomatoes, tomato sauce, green chilies, and taco mix. Combine thoroughly, simmer 10 to 15 min. Place about 1/4 cup mixture in the bottom of a 9x13 baking dish. Place 2 tortillas side by side on the meat mixture. Top each with meat mixture, then cheese. Repeat until each stack contains 6 tortillas layered with meat mixture and cheese. Bake 350 degrees for 20 to 25 min. or until cheese is bubbly. Cut each torte (stack) into quarters with sharp knife before serving. Yield 4 to 6 servings.

Jim and Kathy Peat
Maintenance Supervisor
Will Rogers State Park

"Always remember this, that as bad as we sometimes think our government is run, it's the best run I ever saw."

Eggplant Stew A La Khashayar

1 large eggplant, skin removed and chopped into 1 inch cubes.
2 medium onions, chopped
garlic
1 lb. beef stew meat, chopped
1 teaspoon tumeric
salt and pepper
1 16 oz. can chopped tomatoes
lemon juice
olive oil

Saute eggplant in 1-2 T. olive oil until soft. Remove from pan. Saute onions and garlic in 1 T. olive oil until onions are translucent. Remove from pan. Saute beef stew meat until browned. Add eggplant, onions, garlic, tomatoes and tumeric to meat. Cover and simmer for 30 minutes. Add 1/4 to 1 teaspoon lemon juice to taste, Add salt and pepper to taste, serve with white rice and warm pita bread.

Mike Cramer
Will Rogers Volunteer

Barbecued Trout

To keep fish fresh in appearance and aroma brush inside and out with lemon juice before refrigerating.

Trout marinade:
1/4 c vegetable oil
1/2 c cooking sherry
1/2 c soy sauce
1 T lemon juice
1 clove of garlic, crushed
Blend well before using.

Place trout in a shallow pan and cover with marinade. Let stand at least one hour. Place trout on the grill and barbecue until done, 10-15 minutes.

Jack Thompson
Maintenance Worker 1
Will Rogers State Park

"No man can be condemned for owning a dog. As long as he has a dog he has a friend and the poorer he gets the better friend he has."

Roast Loin of Pork/Orange Sauce with Almond Stuffed Onions

1 pork center loin roast (about 5 pounds)
1/2 clove garlic
1 teaspoon dill weed
1 teaspoon salt

Heat oven to 325 degrees. Rub meat with garlic and dill weed; sprinkle with salt. Place meat fat side up in shallow roasting pan. Insert meat thermometer in center of thickest part of meat, away from fat or bone.
Roast uncovered 2-1/2 to 3 hours to internal temperature of 170 degrees. Allow to stand at room temperature 15 to 20 minutes before carving.

ORANGE SAUCE
1 can (6 oz.) orange juice concentrate
1/2 cup light corn syrup
2 tablespoons catsup

Combine all ingredients in a small sauce pan. Bring to a boil; simmer until slightly thickened. Serve as a sauce over roast pork or use as a glaze during last hour of roasting period.

ALMOND STUFFED ONIONS
6 medium onions, about 3 inches in diameter
3/4 cup coarsely chopped almonds
1-1/2 cups croutons
3/4 teaspoons salt
1/4 teaspoon pepper
1/4 teaspoon sage
1/8 teaspoon thyme
1/4 cup melted butter
1 cup apple juice

Cut a thin slice off root end of each onion; cut a 1/4-inch slice off opposite end. Carefully remove center of each onion with vegetable parer or melon ball cutter, leaving a 3/8-inch shell (at least 3 rings). Arrange onion shells in ungreased 2-quart casserole.

Toss almonds, croutons, salt, pepper, sage, thyme and butter. Fill each onion shell with stuffing. Spoon any remaining stuffing on top of onions. Pour apple juice around onions. Put casserole in oven about 40 minutes before roast pork is done. Bake covered 40 minutes. Uncover and bake until tender, about 20 minutes longer while roast is standing.

Governor Ed Herschler
Governor of Wyoming

Impossible Quiche

1/2 pound bacon or 1/2 pound sausage
1/3 cup sauteed onions
1 cup grated cheese

Put above ingredients in bottom of greased quiche pan.

In the blender put:
2 cups milk (for richer quiche, use light cream)
1/2 cup Bisquick mix
4 eggs
1/2 tsp. salt
black pepper to taste

Pour above mixture into pan on top of the other ingredients. Bake in pre-heated 350 degree oven for 50 - 55 minutes or until center is set. Let stand 5 - 10 minutes before serving.

Marian & Francis Lederer,
Friends of Will Rogers

Eggplant Palmagiano

1 eggplant
8 oz. mozzarella cheese
2 eggs
1/2 cup flour
1/4 tsp. salt
1 tsp. garlic salt
2 tsps. sweet basil
1/3 cup oil
1 pint spaghetti sauce
1 romano cheese

Remove skin of eggplant and slice to about 1/8 to 1/4 inch. Combine flour, salt, garlic salt and sweet basil. Dip each slice into milk, then in flour mixture and lastly in beaten eggs. Fry in oil on each side till golden brown. Spread a bit of sauce on bottom of round pizza pan or baking dish. Spread fried eggplant and top with sauce and sprinkle with romano cheese. Repeat with another layer of eggplant, and romano cheese. Top with sliced mozzarella cheese. Bake at 350 degrees for 15 or 20 minutes or until cheese is melted but not browned. SERVE HOT!

J. Joseph Garrahy
Governor of Rhode Island

91

Herb's Chili Recipe

3 lbs. diced lean beef
1/4 cup olive oil (enough to brown the meat)
6 cups water
6 tablespoons chili powder (3 oz.)
3 teaspoons salt
10 cloves finely chopped garlic
1 teaspoon ground cumin
1 teaspoon marjoram or oregano
1 teaspoon red pepper (cayenne)
1 tablespoon sugar
3 tablespoons paprika (1-1/2 oz.)
3 tablespoons flour
6 tablespoons corn meal
6 chili tepines (or to taste – 1 or 2 make a lot of difference)

Brown meat in hot olive oil in dutch oven or large pot. Add remaining ingredients, stir frequently while simmering over low heat (just enough heat to keep it bubbling). Add corn meal slowly while stiring constantly (so it thickens smoothly). Allow to simmer 2 to 3 hours (until meat is very tender). Add beans and simmer for at least another hour.

2 pounds Pinto beans. Cook separately according to recipe on package. When the beans are added to the chili add liquid from the beans as desired.

Herbert L. Heinze
Calif. State Park Manager IV

Cold Beef Platter-Beuf en Vinaigrette

Cold boiled beef, sliced thin
3 hard boiled eggs

Sauce Vinaigrette
1 tsp. chopped onion
1 tsp. chopped chives
1 tsp. chopped parsley
1 tsp. salt
1/4 tsp. freshly ground pepper
2 Tbls. wine vinegar
3/4 cup salad oil

Mix all the seasoning with the vinegar and allow them to stand several minutes, before combining with oil. Mix thoroughly before serving.

Place the thin slices of cold beef on a deep platter. Cover with slices of hard boiled eggs and pour the viaigrette over it all

This makes a delicious luncheon dish.

Trudy Sandmeier

"Old words is like old friends, you know 'em the minute you see 'em."

Sesame Seed Chicken Wings

3 lbs. chicken wings
1/4 c. flour
1/2 c. cornstarch
1/4 c. sugar
1-1/2 t. salt
1/2 t. MSG
5 t. soy sauce
2 eggs
2 green onions, thinly sliced
2 cloves garlic, crushed
1 T. sesame seeds

Cut wings at the joint and discard the last joint. Combine all other ingredients. Marinate a minimum of two hours. Heat oil to 350 degrees, and fry until golden brown.

Gail and David Sears
District Interpretive Specialist
California State Parks

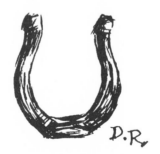

Crab Imperial

1 lb. crabmeat (preferably backfin)
2 tbs. margarine or butter
2 tbs. flour
3/4 cup milk
1 egg, beaten
1 hard-cooked egg, chopped fine
1 tbs. mayonnaise
6 drops Worcestershire sauce
1/2 tsp. dry mustard
1/2 tsp. parsley flakes
1/4 tsp. seafood seasoning
1 tsp. salt
1/4 tsp. pepper
1/2 cup bread crumbs
1/4 cup melted margarine or butter
Pimiento for garnish

Remove cartilage from crabmeat, and put in large bowl. Melt margarine or butter over low heat. Add flour and stir to make paste. Add milk and cook slowly, stirring constantly, until thickened. Reserve 6 tablespoons white sauce; add remainder to crabmeat, along with raw egg, hard-cooked egg, mayonnaise, Worcestershire sauce, mustard, parsley flakes, seafood seasoning, salt and pepper. Mix gently but thoroughly. Put crabmeat mixture into 6 baking shells or ramekins. Top each with bread crumbs, then melted margarine or butter, then reserved white sauce. Add pimiento strips for garnish.

Bake at 350 degrees F., 15 to 20 minutes or until browned on top. Makes 6 servings.

Harry Hughes
Governor, Maryland

Black Beans, NY-TX style

One 1-lb. bag of black ("Turtle") beans   2 tbsp. sherry or vinegar
2 medium-size onions, sliced   clove garlic, sliced
2 sprigs cilantro, chopped   1 sliced carrot
one-half jar picante sauce   1 tsp. cumin

Wash beans and sort out any stones which may have found their way into the package. Place beans in enough water to cover them by 2 inches, and then either soak them overnight, or bring the water to a boil; boil 2 minutes; remove from heat, and let stand for 1 hour. I have tried both methods, and found neither superior to the other. Drain off water; cover beans with enough water to cover them by a few inches; add sherry or vinegar; bring water to boil, cover and simmer for 2 hours. Saute onions, garlic, and carrots together in olive oil, then add it all to the beans. Now you can spend a few precious moments chopping tomatoes, green chilies, and various other goodies, but I have found that it is just as tasty to simply add about 8 oz. of a chunky salsa, the chunkier the better. Add the cumin, the cilantro, a dash of salt, a dash of tabasco or other hot sauce, and a healthy grind of pepper. Cook the beans for another hour. You may find that you have to add water from time to time to keep it from getting too thick; then again, you may like it thick. Best the next day; reheating only improves it. Serve over rice with a dollop of sour cream, or in a bowl; chopped cilantro makes a perfect garnish. Serves 6, or one actor for about a week.

Paul Ukena, Jr. actor
Co-stars as Wiley Post
in THE WILL ROGERS FOLLIES
Understudy for Keith Carradine as
Will Rogers

"I will bet you that this Wiley Post makes it around the world and breaks his own record. I would have liked to have been in there with Post instead of the robot (automatic pilot). And I could have, if I had known as much as it does."

96

Steak Soup

1 stick butter
1 cup flour
1/2 gallon water
1 pound ground beef
1 cup onions, cubed
1 cup carrots, cubed
1 cup celery, cubed
2 cups frozen mixed vegetables
1 can tomatoes
1 Tbls. monosodium glutamate
4 cubes beef bouillon
freshly ground black pepper

Melt butter and add flour to make a smooth paste. Stir in water; set aside.

Saute ground beef, drain grease and add to soup. Parboil the onions, carrots and celery. Add to the ground beef along with the mixed vegetables, tomatoes, monosodium glutamate, beef bouillon and pepper. Bring to a boil, reduce to simmer and cook until vegetables are tender. (Mrs. Alexander freezes this soup.)

Thank you for including the State of Tennessee in the celebration of Will Rogers 100th birthday!

Lamar Alexander
Governor
State of Tennesse

Sweet and Sour Chicken

3/4 Pound chicken breasts,cubed
1 Tablespoon oil
1 Cup green and red pepper strips
1 Tablespoon cornstarch
1/4 Cup Soy sauce
1 Can (8 ounce) chunk pineapple in juice
3 Tablespoons vinegar
3 Tablespoons brown sugar
2 Teaspoon ground ginger
2 Teaspoon garlic powder
1-1/2 Cups instant brown rice

Heat oil in a large skillet,cook chicken until well brown, add peppers, cook and stir 1 to 2 minutes. Mix cornstarch and soy sauce add to pan with pineapple and juice, vinegar, ginger, and garlic powder, bring to a boil. Prepare rice as directed on box. Pour hot chicken over rice.

Nancy Reid
State Park Ranger 1
Topanga State Park

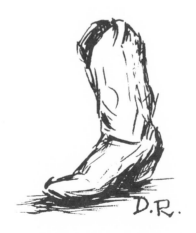

"More's" One Dish Dinner

1-1/2 lbs. of ground round steak
1 package frozen peas or 1 can
1 can whole kernel corn
1-1/2 cups cooked shell macaroni
1 can tomatoes
1 can tomato sauce
1 Tbsp. chili powder

DICE:
2 onions
1 bell pepper
1 can mushrooms
2 small garlic buttons

Saute diced vegetables in small amount of salad oil, add ground meat, salt and pepper to taste, add chili powder. Add 1 can of tomatoes, 1 can tomato sauce. Let simmer for a while, then add peas, corn and cooked macaroni. Empty into a large Pyrex bowl and put cheese on top.

Mrs. William P. Clements, Jr.
First Lady of State of Texas

Spiced Apple Pork Roast

1 boneless pork loin roast, rolled – 4 to 5 pound
1 garlic clove minced
2 Tablespoons flour
1/2 Teaspoon salt
1/2 Teaspoon sugar
1 Teaspoon prepared mustard
Dash of fresh pepper
1 Cup applesauce
1/3 Cup brown sugar
2 Teaspoon vinegar
1/4 Teaspoon ground cloves

Trim all excess fat from pork. Slit the top of the roast and put the minced garlic in the slits. Mix flour, sugar, salt, pepper and mustard. Rub over the roast. Place the meat, fat side up, on a rack in a roasting pan. Bake at 325° for 30 or 40 minutes per pound. Combine applesauce, brown sugar, vinegar and cloves. Brush over roast during the last half hour of baking.

Darea Simolke

Roast Duck with Sausage Stuffing

ROAST DUCK
Night before: Wash ducks thoroughly and place in a glass dish. Stuff each cavity with a celery stalk, 1/4 apple, 1/4 onion, a dash of poultry seasoning and a dash of thyme. Rub outside with salt and seasoned pepper. Pour (at least) a cup of your favorite wine over them, tightly cover, and let marinade overnight in the refrigerator.

Next morning, empty birds (save celery etc.). Stuff with sausage dressing and place in baking pan. Pour all the marinade, including celery, apple etc., over ducks and cook as you would a small baked hen, basting as you go, 350 degrees.

SAUSAGE STUFFING:
Prepare 2 pkg. of Pepperidge Farm herb dressing according to directions. Add one lb. of your favorite sausage (crumbled and well-browned). Add 2 c. chopped celery, 1 c. chopped pecans, 1 c. chopped onions.

This is a favorite recipe of Governor James.

Mrs. Bob James, Junior
The Executive Mansion
Montgomery, Alabama

Souffle de Saumon

Serves 4
Cook in 6-cup souffle mold
1 tsp. butter
2 Tb. plus grated Parmesan cheese
Butter mold and sprinkle with cheese. Preheat oven to 400 degrees.

2 Tb. minced green onions or shallots
3 Tb. butter
3 Tb. flour
1 cup milk (or juice from canned salmon and milk)
1/2 tsp. salt
1/8 tsp. pepper
1 Tb. tomato paste
1/2 tsp. oregano

Cook onions in butter for a moment. Add flour and cook over medium heat for 2 minutes. Remove from heat, beat in liquid all at once, then add seasonings and tomato paste. Boil, stirring, for 1 minute and remove from heat.

4 egg yolks
3/4 cup or more shredded cooked or canned salmon (Oregon Salmon, of course!)
1/2 cup grated Swiss cheese

With pan off of heat, beat in egg yolks one at a time, then add salmon and all but 1 Tbs. cheese. Taste for seasoning.

Glaze with milk or melted butter, or cover surface with plastic wrap. Heat, stirring, to just warm before continuing.

5 egg whites
1/4 tsp. cream of tartar,
pinch of salt

Beat egg whites slowly until they foam, then add cream of tartar and salt. Increase speed gradually and beat until stiff but not dry. Stir one-fourth of egg whites into sauce mixture. Gently *fold* in the rest. Pour into prepared mold and sprinkle with remaining cheese.

Bake in middle level of oven which has been preheated to 400 degrees. Turn oven down to 375 degrees and bake for 30-35 minutes. Check and bake 4-5 minutes after it is golden brown. Souffle is done when skewer comes out clean. Serve *immediately*. Will hold in turned off oven, with door open, for 5 minutes without collapsing.

NOTE: Before baking, souffle may be placed on doubled towel and covered with an inverted large pot for 1 hour.

Victor Atiyeh
Governor
State of Oregon

Casseroles

Spinach Ring

Cook 4 boxes of frozen chopped spinach and drain well. Further chop the spinach in a food processor, or put through a meat grinder. Beat together 4 eggs and 2 egg yolks and add the spinach.

In a sauce pan melt 4 T. butter. Remove the pan from the fire, and stir in 4 T. flour. Return the pan to the fire, and gradually add 1-1/2 c. milk, salt, pepper, and nutmeg to taste. Fill a greased 1-1/4 quart ring mold, and cover the ring with greased waxed paper. Place the ring mold in another pan of hot water. Bake in a 350° oven for about 30 minutes, or until a knife comes out clean when inserted into the spinach. Remove from the oven and from the water, and allow to stand for a couple of minutes before unmolding. The center may be filled with other vegetables.

> Harriet L Axelrad
> Docent, Will Rogers State Park

Will went on a diet of spinach, broiled lamb chops and milk for three days every time he would come home from a trip to lose the weight he would put on.

> Mr. Emil Sandmeier
> former employee of Will Rogers

"Nothing thickens one like travel."

Cowboy Casserole

2 pounds ground beef
8 oz. egg noodles - cooked
1 16 oz. can nibblets whole kernal corn
1 15 oz. can tamales: cut each tamale in thirds
1 small can black olives, sliced
1 can cream of mushroom soup
1 small onion, chopped
1/2 pound cheddar cheese - grated

Brown beef with onions and garlic. Drain off any fat. Mix together all other ingredients, except cheese. Put in a three quart casserole dish, add cheese to top. Bake one hour in a pre-heated oven (350 degrees). Serves 8.

Margaret Cavanagh
Docent, Will Roger State Park

"The short memories of Amercan voters is what keeps our politicians in office."

Mandarin Drumsticks

12 chicken wings
1/2 c. cornstarch
1 egg-slightly beaten
1/4 tsp. salt and 1/4 tsp. seasoned salt
2 Tbs. milk

Cut chicken wings at joint, discard wing tips. Scrape and push meat to one end of the bone, so each piece resembles a small drumstick. In a medium bowl, combine cornstarch, egg, salt, seasoned salt, and milk. Mix well until smooth. Dip each drumstick in batter. Drop in hot grease in a deep freyer or a mini-freyer. Fry until lightly brown. Drain well on paper towel. Place in single layers in a shallow baking pan. Bake at 350 degrees for 30 min. or until chicken is done. Add spicy glaze to chicken and sprinkle with sesame seeds to taste. Return to oven 10 min. Serve hot.

SPICY GLAZE
1 c. granulated sugar
1/4 c water
1/2 c. vinegar
1 tsp. soy sauce
1 Tbsp. catsup
1 Tbsp. chopped green onions (use tops too)

In a small saucepan combine all ingredients. Bring to a boil, stirring until the sugar dissolves.

Donna Raymond
Docent, Will Rogers State Park

"People's minds are changed through observation and not through argument."

Spinach Casserole

2-10 oz. packages chopped frozen spinach, cooked,drained,
1-8 oz. can water chestnuts, sliced
1-8 oz. package shredded cheddar cheese
1 can mushroom soup
1-2^{1}/$_{2}$ oz. can french fried onion rings

In a 9x9 casserole layer one half of the spinach, half of the soup, half the sliced chestnuts, half the onions. Continue, until all the ingredients are used. Put cheese over all.

Bake 350 Degrees (Preheated oven) for 30 min.

Norma P. Barger
Docent, Will Rogers State Park

Macaroni and Cheese Casserole

1 - 7 oz package of macaroni, cooked and drained
2 Cups shredded sharp cheese
1 Can of condensed mushroom soup
1 - 6 oz can mushrooms, sliced and drained
3/4 Cup milk
1/4 Cup chopped onion
1/4 Cup chopped pimento
1/4 Cup chopped green pepper
1/2 of 8-oz package of rich round cheese crackers, crushed
    (1-1/2 cup crumbs)

Combine all ingredients, including 1 cup cracker crumbs. Turn into 2-qt cassarole. Sprinkle with remaining 1/2 cup cracker crumbs. Bake at 325 degrees for 45-50 minutes.

Serves 8.

Colonel Robert and Eloise Gleason.

On August 16th, 1935, with weather conditions just as treacherous as on the preceding day, Robert Gleason, as radio operator, dared with pilot Joe Crosson to fly to Barrow, Alaska, to bring back the bodies of Will Rogers and Wiley Post to Fairbanks, Seattle and finally to Los Angeles.

"Airlines have flown millions of miles and no injuries to anyone. For comparison get the record of some bunch of automobiles . . . You don't have to stop to figure out which is safer. All you have to do is to compare the intelligence of the men that pilot planes with the intelligence of everybody that drives a car."

Noodle Pudding

Boil one half pound of flat noodles.

Wash noodles in cold water and drain.

Mix:
One 12 ounce package of sour cream,
One 8 ounce package of cream cheese (or cottage cheese)
1/4 pound of melted oleo or butter,
1/2 to 3/4 cup of sugar (to taste)

Add:
A dash of cinnamon
Six beaten egg yolks

After noodles have been added to above, fold in six beaten egg whites.

Bake in a greased loaf pan at 350 degrees, until firm. Serve hot. (This pudding can be reheated nicely.)

Variations: Fold in canned fruit, or top with preserved cherries or blueberries or top with nuts and brown sugar or syrup. Great for brunch, lunch, or at a buffet!

> Governor and Mrs. Milton J. Sharp
> State of Pennsylvania

"Some men will stand for a lot of things. But you start taking their women or their jobs away from them and you are going to get something besides platitudes."

Ham Strata

6 slices bread
2 cups cooked, diced ham
1/2 cup chopped onion
1/2 cup chopped celery
1/2 cup green pepper
1/2 cup mayonnaise
1 cup milk
2 eggs
1 can mushroom soup
1 cup grated cheese
1 cup buttered bread cubes
salt and pepper to taste

Saute onion, celery, and green pepper until tender. Combine with diced ham.

Break bread into bite size pieces. Alternate layers of ham mixture and pieces of bread in buttered casserole.

Combine 2 eggs, beaten well, with 1 cup of milk and 1/2 cup mayonnaise. Pour over the casserole.

Refrigerate for several hours or overnight.

Before baking casserole, spread mushroom soup, plus buttered bread cubes, over the mixture and bake uncovered for one hour in 350 degree oven.

Remove from the oven and sprinkle top with a cup of grated cheese. Return to the oven until the cheese is melted.

Either chicken or turkey may be substituted for the ham in this one-dish meal. It may be made in the morning or night before and refrigerated until baking time.

Governor William G. Milliken
State of Michigan

Hamburger Casserole

1-1/2 lbs. hamburger
1/2 cup chopped onion
2 - 8 oz. cans tomato sauce
1 tsp. sugar
1 tsp. salt
1/4 tsp. garlic salt
1/4 tsp. pepper
8 oz. cream cheese
3 cups noodles
1 cup sour cream
1/3 cup green onion
1/4 cup chopped green pepper
Velveeta Cheese

In large skillet, cook meat and onion until meat is lightly brown and onion is tender. Stir in tomato sauce, salt, garlic salt and pepper. Remove from heat. Combine sour cream, cream cheese, green onion and green pepper. Cook noodles according to package and drain. Spread one-half noodles in baking dish, top with some meat mix, cover with cheese mix. Add rest of noodles and meat sauce; top with Velveeta cheese.

Bake at 350 degrees for 30 minutes. Makes 8-10 servings.

Governor and Mrs. J. James Exon
Nebraska

"When you get into trouble five thousand miles from home you've got to have been looking for it."

"Pure Oklahoma" Squaw Corn

4 slices bacon
1 green pepper chopped
1 onion chopped
1 can cream style corn
1 teaspoon salt
4 eggs, beaten

Fry bacon, set aside. Drain all drippings from skillet except 3 tablespoons. Cook and stir green pepper and onion in drippings until onion is tender. Add remaining ingredients. Cook and stir until eggs are thickened throughout, but still moist. Crumble bacon, sprinkle over egg mixture. Four to six servings.

Clem McSpadden
Great Nephew of Will Rogers

Corn and Oysters

1 can cream style corn
2 eggs
1/2 stick margarine
1 cup grated cheddar cheese
1 cup crackers
1 can oysters, drained

Mix corn, eggs, crackers and oysters together and pour into greased baking dish. Dot with margarine and spread grated cheese over top. Bake at 350 degrees about 30 minutes, until set.

Mrs. Clem (Donna) McSpadden
Chelsea, Oklahoma

"The best cure for temperament is hunger. I have never seen a poor temperamental person."

Farcis

(Stuffed vegetables)
Ingredients:
Minced ham
grated cheese
1 egg
1 boiled potato
1 onion
breadcrumbs
seasoning, and garlic to taste
round, ball squash
eggplants
large tomatoes
(Quantities depend on the number and size of vegetables to be stuffed)

Boil the squash and/or eggplants, but not the tomatoes, in salted water with the onion. When tender but still whole, drain and cut in half. Remove soft inside of vegetables and save. Mash up the boiled onion and mix with the ham and add crushed garlic if desired. Mash the potato and inside of vegetables and mix with ham, etc. Mix in some grated cheese. Bind together with beaten egg.

Now fill the squash and eggplants with this mixture, and raw tomatoes if used, from which inside has been removed. Top with cheese and breadcrumbs and cook in hot oven or under grill till brown.

Serve hot, or cold with salad.

Her Serene Highness
Princess Grace of Monaco

Zucchini Casserole

3 strips bacon
2-1/2 Ibs. sliced zucchini squash
1/3 cup chopped celery
1/3 cup chopped onions
1/3 cup chopped green pepper
1 garlic clove minced
1 egg
Bread crumbs

Fry bacon, remove from pan. Saute onions, green pepper, celery, and garlic in bacon drippings until tender. Set aside.

Boil squash till tender, drain and mash well. Crumble bacon, add to squash. Add vegetables and the egg. Mix well together. Pour into a well buttered casserole dish. Line dish with bread crumbs (be generous). Pour in the mixture, top with bread crumbs. Dot with butter. Bake 30 minutes in a 400 degree oven or until top is crusty and brown. Let stand 10 minutes.

Claude Howard
Will Rogers Park

"Live your life so if you lose you are still ahead."

Garden Pizza

2 Pkg. Crescent Rolls (Pillsbury Ready-to-bake)
2 pkg Cream cheese (8 oz. each)
1 c mayonaise
1 tbs. dill
1 tsp. seasoned salt

Line a jelly roll pan with crescent rolls. Bake 375° 11-15 min. until golden brown. Cool. Combine remaining ingredients and spread on crust.

1 cucumber seeded and juiced
3 small tomatoes
1 green and/or red pepper
1/2 bunch broccoli
3 green onions
1/4 lb. fresh mushrooms
black and green olives

Chop (the smaller you chop these the better) the above ingredients and sprinkle on top of cream cheese mixture. Chill. Cut into very small squares and serve.

This is a smash hit for hors d'oeuvres - it will serve a large group. Provide plenty of napkins!

Eleanor Nichols
Docent, Will Rogers State Park

"It ain't taxes that is hurting the country, it's interest."

Chicken Casserole

1-1/2 cup long-grain rice
1 cup milk
8 chicken breasts
1 tsp. salt
1/2 cube butter (melted)
1 can mushroom soup
1 can cream of chicken soup
1 can cream of celery soup

Arrange rice on bottom of casserole (8x11) Pour milk over rice, Layer chicken on top. Mix soups with butter and pour over rice and chicken.

Shake a little paprika on top, bake 275 degrees for 2 hours.

Inez Beye
Docent, Will Rogers State Park

"Everybody is ignorant, only on different subjects."

Spaghetti Casserole

2 large onions chopped
1-1/2 lbs. lean ground beef
1-1/2 teaspoon salt or to taste
1 can Contadina Italian Sauce
1 small can sliced mushrooms
1 24 oz. can V-8 Vegetable juice
1/4 lb. spaghetti (or more)

Saute chopped onion until soft. Add meat and cook until pink color disappears. Add Italian Sauce, mushrooms and vegetable juice. Stir well. Cook slowly about 15 minutes. Add cooked and drained spaghetti. Stir well. Bake in greased casserole at 350 degrees for one hour. Serves 8.

Bea Heiby
Docent, Will Rogers State Park

Spaghetti Western

1 lb ground round steak
1 Large Spanish onion, chopped
1 Zucchini
1 Celery stalk, finely chopped
1/2 Cup red or green pepper, chopped
1/2 lb sliced fresh mushrooms
3 Large cloves garlic, finely chopped
6 or 7 average tomatoes, peeled
1 Large can of tomato puree
1 Cup fresh Basil (or 2 tsp dried Basil)
2 Tsp Oregano
1 Tsp black pepper, coarse
1 Small can of tomato paste
2 Jalapeno peppers (if very hot use only one)

Brown ground steak, draw off and discard any excess grease. Set meat aside. Saute onion, mushrooms, zucchini, celery, red or green peppers and garlic until limp.

In another pot cook down the fresh tomatoes, the tomato puree, tomato paste, Basil, Oregano, black pepper and Jalapeno pepper(s) until thoroughly blended. Then add first saute and ground meat and simmer at least a half hour.

Serve over spaghetti.

Vince Bruce
World Champion Lariat Artist
Star of The Will Rogers Follies

"I was just thinking…it was a little Fourth of July celebration in Claremore…on July Fourth, 1899, they had a steer roping, and I went into it. It was the first one I ever was in; the very first thing I ever did in the way of appearing before an audience in my life… Once you are a showman you are plum ruined for manual labor again."

Spareribs and Sauerkraut

4 Pounds Spareribs
salt and pepper
1 Quart sauerkraut
1/2 Cup apple sauce
2 Tablespoons brown sugar
1 Onion sliced thin
2 Cups water

Cut the ribs and brown them in a skillet, adding salt and pepper.
Pour off the fat. Place the sauerkraut mixed with the apple sauce
and onions in a casserole, place the ribs on top. Pour the water over
the top, cover tightly. Put in a pre-heated oven (350°). Bake 2 hours
or until the ribs are very tender.

Bryan And Frances Sterling
Docents, Will Rogers State Park

Lorri Chamberlin's Sunday Supper

6 Chicken Breasts
2 Cans Cream of Chicken Soup
1 Cup Mayonnaise
1 Cup Cooked Rice
1 tsp. curry (or to taste)
Juice of one lemon
1 Package frozen Broccoli, cooked
1 cup longhorn cheese, grated

Place chicken in a oven proof casserole. Mix next five ingredients
well and put over chicken, put broccoli over mix. Cook in a 350
degree oven until chicken is done, add cheese. Heat until cheese is
melted.

This is a great dish to make a day ahead and heat after church.

Donna Raymond
Docent, Will Rogers State Park

Savory Sausage

2 lbs. bulk sausage
1 cup chopped green pepper
3/4 cup chopped onion
2-1/2 cups chopped celery
1 cup sliced blanched almonds
2 pkgs. Lipton's chicken noodle soup mix (with diced white chicken meat)
4-1/2 cups boiling water
1 cup Minute Rice
1 can water chestnuts chopped

Brown meat, pour off fat. Add green peppers, onion and celery. Saute. Combine soup mix and boiling water in large sauce pan. Stir in rice. Cover and simmer 20 minutes. Add rest of ingredients (sausage mix, almonds and water chestnuts). Stir well. Bake in greased casserole at 375 degrees for 30 minutes.

Serves 8 or 10.

Bea Heiby
Docent, Will Rogers State Park

Cheese Strata

12 slices bread (white preferred)
1/4 tsp. mustard (per slice)
1 lb. Wisconsin cheese, sliced (cheddar)
4 eggs beaten
2 c. milk
1/2 tsp. salt
1/4 tsp. pepper

Preheat oven to 350 degrees. Butter well a 9x13 pan. Place six slices of bread (spread with mustard) in pan. Add a layer of cheese. Repeat. Beat eggs well with milk. Pour egg/milk mixture over bread and cheese. Season with salt and pepper. Bake 30 minutes. Cut in squares and serve warm, as an appetizer or snack.

Martin J. Schreiber

Martin J. Schreiber
Governor
State of Wisconsin

Scalloped Idaho Potato and Onion Casserole

3 lbs. potatoes
3 c thinly sliced onions
boiling water
3-1/2 tsp. salt
3 T. butter
2 T. chopped parsley
2 T. flour
1/2 tsp. paprika
1/2 tsp. pepper
2-1/4 c. milk

Preheat oven to 400 degrees. Lightly grease a 2 qt. casserole. Wash, peel and thinly slice potatoes, place in large sauce pan and add onions. Cover potatoes and onions with boiling water, add 2 tsp. salt. Cook covered 5 min., or until slightly tender, drain. Melt butter, stir in flour, paprika and rest of salt. Gradually stir in milk. Bring to boil, stirring, reduce heat and simmer one minute. Layer 1/3 potato and onion mixture. Sprinkle with 1 T. parsley, top with 1/2 sauce. Repeat, ending with sauce. Bake uncovered 35 min. in mod. oven.

Governor John V. Evans
State of Idaho

Baked Beans

1 large can pork and beans
1 can green lima beans (drained)
1 can kidney beans (drained)
1 c celery (chopped)
1 c onion (chopped)
1/2 c brown sugar
1/2 c white sugar
1 lb. smoked ham

Mix all ingredients together and bake in a slow oven. 200 degrees
250 degrees for 5 hours.

Governor John V. Evans
State of Idaho

Paula Stone Sloan (Fred Stone's daughter) laughed about Will. Her
mother made some beans for him and apologized because they weren't the
best but he said "there never was a bad bean."

"Barba Giuan", or Rissoles

1. Make short pastry with 250 grams flour, 100 grams margarine or butter, water, and salt.

2. Mince and boil Swiss chards.

3. Brown a minced onion in a saucepan, and mix with boiled Swiss chard, one egg, Parmesan cheese, salt and pepper.

4. Roll pastry into a thin sheet which you cut into round pieces (the size of a glass will do), and on the half of each round put a teaspoonful of the mixture. Then fold pastry as in apple turn-overs, and seal with egg yolk.

5. Fry the rissoles in oil, and serve hot with tomato sauce.

Her Serene Highness
Princess Grace of Monaco

"My ancestors didn't come on the Mayflower, *but they met the boat."*

Buddy Rogers' Eggplant Supreme

Slice an unpeeled eggplant into 1/2 inch thick slices.

Dip into salted tomato juice.

Roll in soy flour and place in layers in an oiled casserole.

Chop 2 cloves of garlic and 1 onion fine.

Mix with small can of cream style corn and one can solid tomatoes. Add salt

Pour mixture over eggplant.

Cover with grated Tillamook cheese, and bake in 350 degree oven for one hour.

Mary Pickford

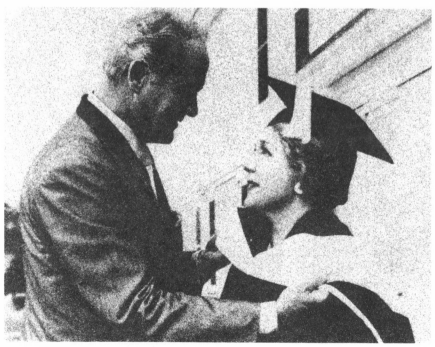

Green Bean Casserole

2 lbs. string beans, fresh or frozen
1 can water chestnuts, drained and sliced
1 can bamboo shoots
2 cans mushroom soup
2 oz. grated cheddar or parmesan cheese

Layer all in buttered casserole, making two layers. Salt and pepper each. Bake 25 minutes at 400 degrees. Remove and sprinkle 1 can french fried onion rings over top. Put back in oven for 5 minutes. Serves 8.

Mrs. James B. Rogers (Astrea)

"The best way to judge just how good a man is, is to find out how he stands around his home and among his kind of people."

Salmon Patties With Potato Patches

1 Cup bread crumbs
1 can salmon, well drained
2 eggs beaten
1 scant teaspoon salt
pepper to taste
3/4 cup milk

Mix all the ingredients together well, heat a skillet with butter,drop the mixture by tablespoons full in the hot butter. Brown well on both sides.

Patches
3 medium size potatoes
1 Tablespoon flour
1 Tablespoon fresh parsley, cut fine
1-1/2 Tablespoon onions, grated
1/3 cup milk
salt and pepper to taste

Peel potatoes, grate them and drain them well in a colander. Stir in the flour and milk to make a thin batter, add the salt and pepper, parsley and onions. Fry in a well oiled hot skillet until they are brown on both sides.

Barbara Rodriguez
Office Assistant #2
Will Rogers State Park

Quiche Lorraine

3 eggs, slightly beaten
2 cups light cream (half and half), or low-fat milk
1 cup shredded Swiss cheese
salt and pepper (1/4-1/8 tsp.)
1/2 cup chopped onion
1/2 cup melted margarine or butter
1/2 cup crumbled cooked bacon
1 unbaked 9" deep pie shell
1 green pepper-chopped
1/2 cup chopped chives

Saute onion in butter (don't brown). Combine eggs, cream, cheese, salt and pepper, Add onion, butter, bacon, and green pepper. Pour into pie shell, and sprinkle with paprika. Bake at 400 degrees for 40 minutes.

I have substituted low-fat milk for cream and margarine for butter to cut calories and it tastes the same.

Elyse Keane
Docent, Will Rogers State Park

Sweet Potato Casserole

3 cups cooked, mashed sweet potatoes
1 cup sugar
1 egg
1/2 t. salt
1/2 stick margarine
1 cup sweet milk
1/2 t. vanilla

Mix all ingredients with mixer and pour into 2 qt. casserole dish. Top with the following: 1 cup brown sugar 1/2 stick margarine 1 cup chopped pecans 1/2 cup flour 1/2 t. vanilla

Mix together and pour over sweet potato mixture. Bake at 350 degrees for 25 to 30 minutes. Serves 6 to 8 people.

Gov. Cliff French
Mississippi

131

Spinach Balls

2 - 10 ounce packages frozen chopped spinach, thawed and drained thoroughly
2 cups herb stuffing mix
4 eggs
1 cup Parmesan cheese
3/4 cup melted margarine
1/2 teaspoon thyme
1/8 teaspoon minced garlic
Pepper to taste

Mix all ingredients thoroughly. Chill *at least* 2 hours, overnight if possible. Roll into balls and place on cookie sheet and freeze (transfer to ziplock bags). Bake frozen at 350 degrees for 25 minutes until sizzly. Makes 6 dozen.
YUM!

Dee Hoty
Broadway star
'Betty Blake Rogers' in
The Will Rogers Follies

"On November 25th, 1908, I was married to Betty Blake of Rogers, Arkansas. When I roped her that was the star performance of my life."

Italian Delight

1 small pkg. noodles, boiled in water
1 lb. hamburger, fried. Add 1 large onion, chopped
2 cloves garlic, minced
1/2 c green pepper
1 t parsley
a few pieces Rosemary
salt and pepper to taste

Next add:
1 T Worcestershire sauce, 1/2 can whole kemel corn, 1/2 t tamale pie spice, 2 cans tomato hot sauce (or plain), 2 or 3 slices cheese cut small and 1/2 t Grama's seasoning or chili powder.

Put in greased baking dish and bake 35 minutes.

Ron and Lee Elkins
Chief Ranger
Will Rogers State Park

"I never in my life made a single dollar without having to chew some gum for it."

Grandmother's Corn Pudding

Mix together:
2 T. flour
1/2 t. salt
1/4 cup sugar
Add:
1 can cream style corn (17 oz.)
1 can evaporated milk (5.3 oz.)
1/2 can of regular milk
3 slightly beaten eggs

Pour into a buttered casserole (1-1/2 qt. size). Sprinkle top with 2 tablespoons chopped butter. Place the casserole dish in a pan holding 1 inch of water. Bake at 400 degrees for 3/4 hour and check to see if center is firm. Sometimes it takes an hour.

Governor John N. Dalton
State of Virginia

Salads

Halved Avocados with Hot Cocktail Sauce

6 tablespoons butter or margarine
6 tablespoons catsup
2-1/2 tablespoons each vinegar and water
4 teaspoons sugar
2-1/2 teaspoons worcestershire
1/2 teaspoon salt
dash tabasco
4 small avocados
lobster or crabmeat, or shrimp

In the top of a double boiler, mix together the butter, catsup, vinegar, water, sugar, Worcestershire, salt and Tabasco to taste. Heat over boiling water until butter has melted and sauce is smooth. Cut avocados in half lengthwise, separate halves, and remove seeds. Add shrimp, lobster or crabmeat into hollow of avocado before covering liberally with hot sauce. Serve on a bed of lettuce leaves. Garnish with lemon wedge and serve as an appetizer. Makes 8 servings.

Footnote: Double recipe for sauce because you'll like it and wish you had made more. This particular sauce is great with any kind of whitefish. Will keep for weeks if refrigerated.

Mike O'Callaghan
Governor of Nevada

"Mary E. Carr's" Three Rice-Walnut Salad

5 cups water
1 tsp. salt
1/2 cup wild rice, rinsed
1/4 cup brown rice
1/4 cup white rice
1 medium onion, thinly sliced
1 cup celery, sliced
1 cup red grapes, halved
1 cup green grapes, halved
1 cup walnut pieces
1/2 cup raisins
1/4 cup parsley-chopped

Combine wild rice, salt, and water, simmer twenty minutes. Add brown rice, simmer covered twenty minutes, add white rice, simmer covered twenty minutes. Let stand ten to twenty minutes, off heat. Drain completely. Put in a dish and chill thoroughly. Mix all other ingredients and toss with dressing

Dressing
1 tsp. salt
1/4 tsp. pepper
1 tsp. coarse mustard
1/4 cup walnut oil
2 tsp. white wine vinegar

Emil Sandmeier
Docent, Will Rogers State Park

"Live your life so that whenever you lose it, you are ahead."

139

"Grandpa's" Salad Dressing

2 cups Wesson oil
1 cup cold water
1/2 cup seasoned rice vinegar
3 tsp. Heinz Chili Sauce
3 tsp. Heinz Sweet Relish
2 tsp. prepared Dijon mustard
2 tsp. Maggi seasoning
Salt to taste
1/4 tsp. Fresh ground black pepper

Mix all ingredients in blender - makes about one quart. - Keep refrigerated.

When preparing the salad green, use a generous amount of chopped parsley and onion.

Emil Sandmeier
Docent, Will Rogers State Park

"I got one little old soft flat red grip, Or bag, that if I tell it when I am leaving it will pack itself. And that Emil packs a dozen of everything."

Tapioca Salad

Soak 1 pkg. (large) tapioca in 4 cups water from 5-12 hours. Drain.

Cook in 2-1/4 cups milk on top of double boiler until soft (at least 30-45 min.).

Whip 1 cup cream and add 3/4 cup sugar. Drain 1 can fruit cocktail and cut up 1/2 jar maraschino cherries.

Cool tapicoa to luke warm and add cream (whipped) and the fruit. Stir well and chill.

Governor Harvey Wollman
State of South Dakota

24-Hour Layer Salad

Iceberg lettuce torn in bite-size pieces
1/2 green pepper, chopped
1/2 red pepper, chopped
1/2 cup celery, chopped
1/2 sweet red Spanish onion (other onions are too strong)
1 package frozen peas
1-1/2 cups mayonnaise
2 tablespoons sugar
4 ounces grated cheddar cheese
8 slices of crisp fried bacon, crumbled

Line a 13x9x2 Pyrex dish with bite-size pieces of crisp iceberg lettuce. Sprinkle with chopped green pepper and chopped red pepper. If red pepper is not available, use the other half of the green pepper. Add a layer of chopped celery, then a layer of chopped sweet red Spanish onion, and a layer of uncooked frozen peas. Combine the sugar and mayonnaise. Spread over these ingredients. Sprinkle top with grated cheddar cheese. Top the salad with crumbled bacon. Refrigerate overnight.

Serves 10 to 12.

Robert F. Bennett
Governor-State of Kansas

Shrimp Salad

3 pounds cooked, chopped shrimp
6 hard boiled eggs, chopped
chopped olives
1 cup chopped celery
juice of 3 lemons
salt and pepper
mayonnaise

To chopped shrimp add eggs, olives and celery; lemon juice, salt and pepper to taste and mayonnaise. Chill. Serves 9 to 12.

James B. Edwards
Governor, State of South Carolina

Cottage Cheese Jello Salad

1 small carton cottage cheese
1 small package Jello-(lemon or orange)
1 small can crushed pineapple or mandarin oranges
1 small cool whip

Put cottage cheese in the bottom of a 9x9 pan. Sprinkle dry Jello over cottage cheese. Mix in the drained fruit and the cool whip. Stir well, pour over cottage cheese and Jello. Let it set in the refrigerator for at least four hours.

Norma P. Bargar
Docent, Will Rogers State Park

Cucumber and Pineapple Salad

1/2 cup vinegar
Juice of 1 lemon
1/4 cup sugar
1/4 teaspoon salt
2 tablespoons gelatin (2 envelopes)
1/4 cup cold water
1 cup hot water
1 cup crushed pineapple
1 cup diced cucumbers (peeled)
(use medium size cucumber)

Soak gelatin in cold water. Add hot water. Add vinegar, sugar and salt. Grease individual molds with Wesson Oil. When beginning to set, add pineapple and cucumber. Put into molds. Place in refrigerator. *Must cover with wax paper.* Makes 12-15.

Governor James B. Hunt, Jr.
State of North Carolina

Vermicelli Salad

6 oz. vermicelli, cooked and drained (pasta)
1/3 C. red wine vinegar
1/3 C. salad oil
1 clove garlic, minced
1/4 tsp. salt
1/4 tsp. dried basil, crushed
1/8 tsp. pepper

Combine these ingredients in a jar and shake to make the dressing. Toss half of the dressing with the cooked pasta. Cover and chill.

2 6 oz. jars marinated artichoke hearts, drained and chopped
1 C. sliced fresh mushrooms

Toss remaining dressing with the artichokes and mushrooms. Cover and chill.

Before serving, toss the two mixtures together. Add two tomatoes, chopped, and 2 T. snipped parsley. Salt and pepper to taste.

This is delicious as a side dish with chicken and turkey. Or, add 2 cups of cut-up cooked chicken or turkey to the salad. It's good to take on a picnic - great at the Hollywood Bowl.

Carol Sandmeier
Volunteer, William S. Hart Ranch

"Steve's" Potato Salad

6 potatoes
1-1/2 cup mayonnaise
1/2 cup salad dressing
1/2 cup pickle relish
1/4 cup chopped red onion
2 Tbls prepared mustard
1/4 cup chopped celery
2 hard boiled eggs

Cover potatoes with cold water, cook until tender, peel while the potatoes are still very hot. Mix all other ingredients well. Fold into the potatoes (sliced or chopped)

The Greek's Place
Claremore, Oklahoma

"There is nothing like congenial friends to just sit around with nothing in particular to knock and a good word for all."

Spinach Salad

Serves 8

Large bunch of fresh spinach
2 hard boiled eggs, chopped
1 can water chestnuts
6 strips of bacon – cooked, crumbled (use more if you wish)
1 can bean sprouts (if fresh, use 1/2 pound)
Mix together with dressing by tossing lightly.

DRESSING 1/2 cup white sugar
1/3 cup ketchup
1/4 cup vinegar
1/2 cup salad oil
2 tablespoons of Worchestershire sauce
pinch of basil or lemon pepper

> James R. Thompson
> Governor, Illinois

Larry Beye's Chicken Salad

3 chicken breasts, cooked and shredded
1/2 head of cabbage, shredded
2 green onions, chopped
1/2 c. sliced almonds
2 Tbsp. toasted sesame seeds
2 pkgs. Top Ramen Noodles, soaked in hot water to soften

Dressing:
2 Tbsp. sugar
1/2 c. salad oil
2 Tbsp. vinegar
1 Tbsp. salt
1/2 Tsp. pepper

Mix everything together and set in the refrigerator for one day.

Inez Beye
Docent, Will Rogers State Park

Chicken Fruit Salad

3 cups cooked chicken - cut in chunks - bite size
3/4 cup chopped celery
3/4 cup grapes (red, halved and seedless)
20 oz. can pineapple chunks in syrup
11 oz. can mandarin oranges, drained
1/4 cup salad dressing (Best Foods)
Lettuce Leaves
1/4 cup chopped pecans

Toss chicken, celery, grapes, pineapple, manderin oranges, and 3 Tbls. chopped pecans.

Gently mix in salad dressing, with the chicken mixture, chill.

Lemon Honey Dressing
1/2 cup honey
1/2 cup lemon juice
1/4 tsp. salt
1/4 cup sherry
2 Tbls. sesame seeds

Blend all ingredients together. Chill and keep refrigerated before serving.

Marjorie Hanson
Docent, Will Rogers State Park

Avocado Ring

1 pkg. lemon flavored gelatin
1 c. boiling water
1 c. sour cream
1 c. mayonnaise
1 c. mashed avocado

Pour boiling water over gelatin and stir until dissolved, cool. Add sour cream, mayonnaise and avocado–turn into 8 inch ring mold which has been rinsed in cold water. Chill. Unmold and garnish with watercress, red grapes and unpeeled apple slices. Serves 8.

Helen McSpadden Eaton
(niece of Will Rogers)
Chelsea, Oklahoma

D.R.

"I can't tell you where to write for I don't know where I will be."

Sauces

"It's The Pits Of Claremore" Salsa

1 #10 can whole peeled tomatoes
2 tsp. salt
3/4 tsp. crushed garlic
3/4 tsp. crushed black pepper
3/4 tsp. cumin
1/2 cup diced Jalapeno peppers
3/4 cup diced onions
1/2 cup cilantro chopped

Grind tomatoes to chunks (do not puree). Blend in other ingredients, cover and refrigerate. Use as needed, makes about one gallon.

Ashley, and Dad
Jim May
"It's The Pits"
Bar B.Q. Restaurent
Claremore, Oklahoma

"The Man With A Message Is A whole lot harder to listen to."

California Shrimp with Mandarin Oranges

2-1/2 pound cooked shrimp
2 medium sweet onions, peeled and sliced thinly
1 can mandarin oranges
1-1/2 cups cider vinegar
1/2 cup extra virgin olive oil
1 clove garlic, crushed
1/2 tsp. pepper
2 tsp. mustard seed
5 tsp. sweet pepper flakes
2 tsp. chopped parsley
1/2 tsp. dried crushed red pepper
1/2 cup catsup
2/3 cup lemon juice
1/4 cup sugar
2 tsp. salt (or to taste)
1 tsp. celery seed

Place shrimp, onions, and oranges in a large mixing bowl. Mix all of the rest of the ingredients well and pour over shrimp. Cover and marinate 2 to 3 days, stirring each day.

Drain and serve as a salad or appetizer. Serves 12 as an appetizer.

Mary Weiss
Docent, Will Rogers State Park

Wilder Ranch Fiesta Salsa

Chop four medium tomatoes

Add:
Three tomatillos, chopped
Two cloves of garlic, minced
One half medium onion, chopped

Add peppers (may be roasted first):
One California or Aneheim
One Patilla or Ancho
One Jalapeno

Add two or three sprigs of cilantro. Mix and salt to taste.

Note: Salsa can be varied by peppers used. Jalapeno and serranos for more heat, Anaheims and Pattila for less heat.

Randy Sederquist,
Chief Ranger, Topanga Sector,
Santa Monica Mountains District

Grandpa's Guacamole

All you need for preparation is a potato grater (for hash browns) a knife and a teaspoon.

Select one medium size avocado
grate 1/4 onion (medium size)
grate 1/4 tomato (medium size)

Spoon out the avocado and chop it with the teaspoon.

Add:
1/2 teaspoon chopped parsley
1/2 teaspoon Maggi seasoning
add a little lemon juice and a little olive oil
Mix the whole thing with the teaspoon and Pronto - your guacamole is ready.

> Emil Sandmeier
> Docent, Will Rogers State Park

"We got a fellow named Emil. He has got some other name but you can't pronounce it. Emil is all I know. Well he kinder runs the Rogers household. He is of that capable tribe called the Swiss, they can speak anything, and can do anything."

Cowboy Dip

1/2 pound ground beef
1 can stewed tomatoes
1 medium onion, chopped
1 large jar cheez whiz
2 tsp. worcestershire sauce
1 tsp. salt
1 tsp. oregano
1 Tbls. Bitters

Brown beef, add tomatoes, onions,and seasonings. Blend in cheese and simmer mixture, uncovered 20 to 30 minutes. Serve with chips or raw vegetables.

Donna McSpadden, (Mrs.Clem)
Chelsea, Oklahoma

"My ancestors didn't come over on the Mayflower, but they met the boat."

FLO ZIEGFELD WINDOW
WILL ROGERS RANCH HOME
SANTA MONICA CALIF

Appetizers
and
Beverages

Liver Pate

1/2 stick butter, melted
1/2 pound chopped mushrooms
1 small onion, chopped
1 clove garlic, chopped
1/2 tsp. salt
1/2 tsp. fresh ground pepper
1 8 oz. cream cheese
1 pound Braunschweiger

Add mushrooms to melted butter. Saute, add onion, garlic, salt and pepper. Add the cream cheese and Braunschweiger. Blend well in blender. Pack in 2 or 3 plastic tubes and refrigerate or freeze.

Dorothy and Irv Gordan
Docent, Will Rogers State Park

"Even when you're on the right track, you'll get run over if you just sit there."

"Razmatasle"

2 ears of fresh corn, cut off the cob, scrape the cob to get the milk.
1/2 medium onion, finely chopped
1/2 medium tomato, finely chopped
2 tsp. seasoned rice vinegar
1/2 tsp. salt
1/2 tsp. Maggi seasoning
8 to 10 turnes on the pepper mill

Mix well together.

Emil Sandmeier,
Docent, Will Rogers State Park

Tomato Juice Cocktail

1 peck ripe tomatoes
1 large onion
2 buttons garlic
1/4 cup vinegar
2 tablespoons salt
1 tablespoon celery salt
4 dashes Tabasco sauce
1/2 teaspoon salycilic acid

Method: Wash and quarter tomatoes, cook without adding water until well done. Add onion and garlic just before removing from fire and rub through colander. Put in kettle again, adding remaining ingredients. Heat to boiling point and seal in sterilized jars.

Maude Rogers Lane
(sister of Will Rogers)
Chelsea, Oklahoma

Irish Coffee O'Callaghan Style

Freshly ground coffee, fairly strong
One jigger Irish whiskey per cup of coffee

Top each serving with sweet whipped cream and grated chocolate if desired. Serve in heavy pre-warmed mugs.

Governor Mike O'Callaghan
State of Nevada

"Canada is a mighty good neighbor and a mighty good customer. That's a combination that is hard to beat."

"Plains Special" Cheese Ring

1 pound grated sharp cheese
1 cup finely chopped nuts
1 cup mayonnaise
1 small onion, finely grated
Black pepper
Dash cayenne
Strawberry preserves, optional

Combine all ingredients except preserves, season to taste with pepper; Mix well and place in a 5 or 6 cup lightly greased ringmold. Refrigerate until firm for several hours or overnight. To serve, unmold, and if desired, fill center with strawberry preserves, or serve plain with crackers.

With best wishes,
President & Mrs. Jimmy Carter
The White House

"Plains Special" Cheese Ring

1 pound grated sharp cheese
1 cup finely chopped nuts
1 cup mayonnaise
1 small onion, finely grated
Black pepper
Dash cayenne
Strawberry preserves, optional

Combine all ingredients except preserves, season to taste with pepper. Mix well and place in a 5 or 6 cup lightly greased ring mold. Refrigerate until firm for several hours or overnight.
To serve, unmold, and if desired, fill center with strawberry preserves, or serve plain with crackers.

With best wishes, Rosalynn Carter

"No matter what a President does, he is wrong according to some people. . . . "

165

Mike's Mushrooms

8 Mushrooms
8 oz.cream cheese
3 tsp. Bacon bits
1/4 cup lemon juice
Dash cayenne pepper
1/4 cup chopped parsley
3 garlic buds, chopped
Sliced American cheese

Clean mushrooms and take out the stems. Mix well together, all ingredients. Fill mushrooms, put a slice of cheese on each mushroom. Put in a pre-heated oven (350 degrees) for 20 minutes. Use a Pyrex dish, put mushrooms in flat, do not stack.

"Mushroom Topping"
1/2 cup butter
2 Tbls. Chives
1/4 cup Chopped parsley
3 garlic buds, minced
2 Tbls. Lemon Juice
Salt and pepper to taste

Mix all well, cook until butter is melted. Before serving pour the mix over the mushrooms and heat till warm.

Bryan and Frances Sterling

"I'd rather be right then Republican."

Soups

Creme Sénégalaise

3 tablespoons butter
2 medium size green apples
2 stalks celery
2 medium size onions
2 teaspoons curry powder
2 teaspoons flour
1 quart chicken bouillon
salt
pepper
nutmeg
1 pint light cream (or evaporated milk)
1/2 cup white meat of chicken
paprika

Melt 3 tablespoons butter. Add two medium size green apples, peeled, cored and diced small; 2 stalks of celery finely chopped; and 2 medium size onions, grated. Cook until just beginning to take on yellowish color, stirring constantly; then sprinkle 2 teaspoons of curry powder (more if desired), mix with 2 teaspoons of flour. Continue cooking for 2 or 3 minutes longer, stirring constantly.

Gradually stir in 1 quart of chicken bouillon and bring to boil. Reduce the flame, and let simmer gently for 45 to 50 minutes. Empty the whole contents of the pan into a fine mesh sieve and rub through. Cool, after seasoning to taste with salt, pepper and a dash of nutmeg.

When cold, stir in 1 pint of light cream or undiluted evaporated milk and 1/2 cup of finely diced white meat of chicken.
Chill in refrigerator for 3 hours and serve in chilled soup plates, with garnish of sprinkling of paprika.

This is a cold chicken soup and one of our most favorite dishes.

Best wishes for the 100th birthday anniversary celebration of Will Rogers.

Evelle J. Younger
Former Attorney General
State of California

Bean Soup

3 slices bacon
2 c. baked or boiled beans
4 c. cold water
1 Tbsp. flour
1 Tbsp. butter
Salt, pepper, paprika (to taste)

Cook bacon, add to beans. Add water, cook until mushy. Press through strainer. Add a little water if needed. Beans should not be too thick. Thicken with flour and butter. Add seasonings to taste.

On one of the many visits to the Roger Ranch, Mrs. Stone saw Will walking around eating some beans with a shoehorn. She offered to get him a spoon. Will replied that he was doing just fine and went on eating.

Mrs. Fred Stone
(Given by Mrs. Paula Sloane,
Fred Stone's daughter)

Gumbo

1/2 Pound bacon
1/2 Cup chopped scallions & tops
2 Large onions
1 Large clove garlic (minced)
1 Bell pepper (minced)
4-5 Tablespoons plain flour
5 Cups water
2 Teaspoons salt
1 Teaspoons dried thyme
1/4 Teaspoon coarse ground black pepper
2 (1 lb. cans) tomatoes and liquid
2 Bay leaves
2 Tablespoons fresh parsley
2 Packages frozen okra
2 Cups diced ham
1 Teaspoon creole seasoning (optional)
3 Drops Tabasco
2 Pounds cooked shelled shrimp
1 Pound fresh or frozen crab meat
1 Teaspoon gumbo file powder (optional)

In a large soup kettle or Dutch oven, saute bacon until crisp; remove bacon, crumble and reserve. In bacon drippings, saute onions, scallions, garlic and bell pepper. Add flour. Brown to make "roux". Gradually add water, salt, thyme, pepper, tomatoes, bay leaves and parsley. Cover pot and simmer slowly for two hours. Add okra, diced ham, creole seasoning and Tabasco and simmer 15 minutes. Add shrimp and crab meat and simmer uncovered 10 minutes. Just before serving, add one tablespoon gumbo powder. Spoon hot fluffy rice in serving bowls. Ladle gumbo over rice. Sprinkle with bacon bits and serve.

Georgia's coastal waters furnish a delicious bounty. Shrimp, crab and salt water fish are caught in abundance the year round.

Reservoirs, ponds and streams offer bass, trout and pan fish. The State is rapidly becoming a leading producer of catfish on a commercial basis.

Governor and Mrs. George Bushu
State of Georgia

Corn Chowder

1 stick butter
2 cups onions, chopped fine
4 cups corn (cream style)
1 cup green peppers (chopped fine)
–if you like peppers–
2 cups milk
1 cup whipping cream

Saute onions and butter together. Add cream style corn and milk
and cream. Add salt and seasoning, salt to taste. (Add green peppers
if desired.)

Governor James A. Rhodes
State of Ohio

*"Don't sell America short. Get some good stock and hold it till it's worth
more, then sell, but don't gamble."*

174

Hamburger Minestrone Soup

1 lb. ground beef
1 cup fresh onions, chopped fine
1 cup potatoes, chopped small
1 cup carrots, chopped small
1/2 cup celery, chopped small
1/2 cup cabbage, chopped small
No. 2 can tomatoes
1/4 cup rice
1 bay leaf
1/2 tsp. thyme leaves
1/4 tsp. basil leaves
5 tsp. salt
1/2 tsp. pepper
1-1/2 qts. water

Brown beef and onions. Add potatoes, carrots, celery, cabbage, tomatoes, rice and seasonings. Then add water, cover and simmer for 1 hour. Sprinkle with cheddar or parmesan cheese. Serves 5.

Mrs. James B. Rogers (Astrea)

Clam Chowder

Several quarts of clams or quahogs
2 cups of water (broth)
1/4 lb. butter
1-3/4 cups thinly sliced onions
2 tbsp. flour
2-1/2 cups potatoes cut into 1/2″ cubes
2 cups celery, coarsely chopped
1 bay leaf, quartered
2-1/2 tsp. salt
1/2 tsp. Accent
1/4 tsp. pepper
4 cups milk
1 cup medium cream
1 cup sour cream

Saute onions in 5 tsps. butter approximately five minutes. Remove from heat. Add flour and mix. Gradually add broth. Add potatoes, celery, seasonings and most of clams. Simmer until potatoes are tender.
Scald milk, remove from heat. Add cream and sour cream. Beat with beater until smooth. Reheat slowly (don't boil). Add to potato mixture with rest of clams. Heat five minutes. Remove bay leaf pieces and top with remaining butter.

I am enclosing a copy of my favorite recipe for clam chowder which I hope you will enjoy as much as I do.

Michael S. Dukakis
State of Massachusetts

Potato Soup With Sausage

1 lb. sausage links, cut in 1/4 inch slices
1 cup celery sliced
1/2 cup chopped onions
1/2 teaspoon dried thyme
1/2 teaspoon salt
2 tablespoons all-purpose flour
1 can chicken broth (15 ounce can)
1/2 cup water
4 potatoes pared and diced(about 4 cups)
1 cup milk
1 cup sliced green beans, partially cooked
Fresh chopped parsley

In a heavy skillet brown sausage, remove sausage and set aside. Drain all but 1 tablespoon of the fat, saute celery, onions, thyme and salt. Cook until onion is tender. Stir in flour, gradually add broth and water, stirring until mixture comes to a boil. Add potatoes; cover and cook 25 minutes, or until potatoes are tender. Allow soup to cool. Puree 2 cups of the cooled soup in a blender. Return to kettle, add the milk, beans and sausage, heat until soup is hot. Garnish with parsley.

Don Raymond
Illustrater, Will Rogers Cookbook

D.R.

Bay Country Crab Soup

1 pound beef shin, bone-in
3 quarts water
1 large onion, chopped
2 large stalks celery, chopped
1 1-pound can tomatoes
1 tablespoon salt
1/4 teaspoon black pepper
1/8 teaspoon cayenne pepper
1 10-ounce package frozen mixed vegetables
1 package fresh or frozen mixed soup vegetables
1 pound Maryland regular crabmeat
1/2 pound Maryland claw crabmeat

Put first 8 ingredients in a large pan and simmer, covered, until meat is very tender, about 3 hours. Add rest of ingredients and simmer, covered, until vegetables are done. Makes about 5 quarts soup.

Harry Hughes
Governor, Maryland

Breads

Basic Sourdough Recipe

Into the Sourdough dump sugar, egg and oil. Mix well. Add soda the last thing when ready for batter to hit the griddle. Dilute soda in 1 tbsp. of warm water. Fold gently into Sourdough. *Do not beat.* Notice deep hollow tone as Sourdough fills with bubbles and doubles bulk. Bake on hot griddle to seal brown. Serve on hot plate.

Governor Jay S. Hammond
State of Alaska

"This Alaska is a great country."

Hot Water Cornbread

1-1/2 c. white cornmeal
1/2 Tsp. salt
3/4 c. boiling water

Bacon grease for frying, (oil or other shortening can be used). Mix cornmeal and salt in a pan with handle for holding. Pour in boiling water gradually beating constantly. When smooth, shape into flat pones. Fry in about one inch deep grease until lightly browned and crisp. Makes 8-12 pones.

Thelma Bacon
Member of the Pocahontas Womans
Club of Claremore, Oklahoma

Squaw Bread

2 c. flour
1 tsp. sugar
1/2 tsp. salt
1 c. milk
4 tsp. baking powder

Mix and roll like biscuits. Cut in 2x4 inch pieces and slit center. Fry in deep fat until golden brown.

Gladys Bell
Member of the Pocahontas Womans
Club of Claremore, Oklahoma

Zucchini Date/Nut Bread

2 cups pecans
4 eggs
2 cups brown sugar
1 cup vegetable oil
2-1/2 cups whole wheat flour
1 cup white flour
1-1/2 tsp. baking soda
1/2 tsp. nutmeg
1 tsp. cinnamon
3/4 tsp. baking powder
2 cups grated zucchini
1 cup dates
1 tsp. vanilla

Beat eggs, add sugar, then oil. Combine all dry ingredients and add to first mixture. Add squash. Stir in vanilla.
Grease 2 pans (9x5x2 inch).

Bake 350 degrees for 1-1/4 hrs. (or till done). Let stand for 10 minutes. Turn out on racks to cool. Serves 12.

Lew Ayres

Mr. Ayres made State Fair with Will Rogers in 1933.

"No matter how late you are, you are never too late for pictures."

Leola's Cornbread

1-1/2 cups buttermilk
1/2 teaspoon soda, stirred into milk
1 egg
2 teaspoons baking powder
1 teaspoon salt
1 teaspoon sugar
3 tablspoons bacon drippings
3/4 cup meal

Melt drippings in skillet and when it is hot, pour in mixture.

Beat till smooth.

Bake at 450 degrees until done and brown. (About 20 minutes or a little more depending on the shape of the pan.)

Note: If the sheet of batter is thin, it doesn't take as long as a thick layer in a smaller pan.

Governor David Pryor
State of Arkansas

Fayetteville, Ark., Feb. 22.– –
"Say, if you want to visit the most beautiful country in the United States, don't overlook these Ozark Mountains. In these are where I grabbed off my only wife. So you will pardon me for bragging on Arkansas."

Florida Orange Bread

3/4 cup Florida orange rind (about 4 oranges)
1-1/2 cups sugar
1/3 cup water
3 tablespoons butter
1-1/2 cups orange juice
3 eggs, well beaten
4 cups sifted all-purpose flour
4 teaspoons baking powder
1/2 teaspoon soda
1 teaspoon salt

Remove the thin orange rind with a sharp knife, cutting around the orange; cut rind into very thin slivers with scissors or knife. Combine sugar and water; add rind; stir constantly over heat until sugar is dissolved; cook slowly 5 minutes. (The peel and syrup should measure 1-1/3 cups).

Add butter, stir until melted; add orange juice and beaten eggs. Sift together into mixing bowl flour, baking powder, soda and salt. Add orange mixture and mix just enough to moisten ingredients (batter should be lumpy). Bake in greased and lined loaf pan 9x5x3″ in slow oven (325 degrees) 1 hour and 15 minutes. Turn out on rack to cool. Yield – 1 loaf.

Governor Reubin Askew
State of Florida

"The higher up our officials get, the less they seem to know about human nature."

Self Rising Bread

3 c self-rising Flour (Gold Medal)
2 T sugar
1 12 oz. can Beer at room temperature
Melted Butter, to top the loaf

Mix together dry ingredients. Add beer 1/3 at a time. Mix well. Pour into a well greased pan. Dribble butter over the bread. Half way through the baking, dribble more butter. Bake 1 hour at 350 degrees. Makes 1 loaf pan 9x4x3, 2 medium small, or 3 small pans.

Mary Olivera
Docent, Will Rogers State Park

"A bunch of American tourists were hissed and stoned yesterday in France but not until they had finished buying."

"Jane and Dick's" Popovers

1 cup flour
1 cup cold water
2 eggs
1/2 tsp. salt

Butter generously 4 or 5 deep muffin tins or glass custard cups. Beat all ingredients together with rotary beater until smooth. Pour mixture into greased muffin tins or custard cups. Fill them 2/3 full. Place in a cold oven. Turn oven to 425 degrees. Bake until golden brown, 40 or 50 minutes.

Jan Forbath,
Docent, Will Rogers State Park

"Live your life so if you lose it you are still ahead."

Banana Nut Bread

2 cups Bisquick
1 cup granulated sugar
2 teaspoon baking soda
2 large banana's (very ripe)
1/4 cup black walnuts (any nut can be used) chopped
2 eggs
1/3 cup buttermilk or sour cream

Mix sugar and baking soda, combine with the Bisquick, mix well. Add all the other ingredients, beating the eggs slightly first. Mix together well. Put in a well greased 9x15 loaf pan. Bake 40 to 45 minutes in a pre-heated 350° oven.

Keith Carradine-Actor
Stars as Will Rogers
Will Rogers Follies

"Well, all I know is just what I read in the papers. The old paper in the morning is my breakfast. 'Course, I don't entirely depend on it. I like it to be accompanied by some ham and eggs, and a few biscuits, a series of cups of coffee, a few wheat cakes to help get your mind off the editorials.

So, with my California grapefruit, raised in Laredo, Texas, I like a paper that's liable to blurt out with the truth, even if they step on a Republican."

Will Rogers Centennial
Celebration Corn Bread

1 cup yellow corn meal
1 cup flour
1 Tablespoon baking powder
1 tablespoon sugar
1 teaspoon salt
1/3 cup soft butter
1 large egg (or two small)
1 cup milk

Combine all dry ingredients, mix well. Add butter, blend well. Add egg and milk. Mix all together until just blended. Pour into well buttered 8˝ square pan. Bake in hot oven (400 degrees) 25 minutes.

Donna Raymond
Docent, Will Rogers State Park

D.R.

"Old words is like old friends, you know 'em the minute you see 'em."

Corn Meal Pancakes

1 cup flour (sifted)
1/2 cup corn meal
2-1/2 teaspoons baking powder
1/2 teaspoon salt
2 eggs
1 cup milk
2 Tablespoons shortening (fresh bacon fat is good)

Separate eggs; beat whites until stiff but not dry. Sift dry ingredients together; stir egg yolks into milk and add to egg whites, then stir in dry ingredients and shortening. Mix only enough to blend. Drop on a moderately hot griddle (375 degrees) and turn once when pancakes are bubbly on top. Serve immediately with butter and New Hampshire maple syrup.

I am honored to be included in this project and pleased to enclose a recipe that is often served at our Mt. Cube Farm in Oxford, New Hampshire.

I am looking forward to visiting the Will Rogers State Historic Park.

Meldrim Thomson, Jr.
Governor – State of New Hampshire

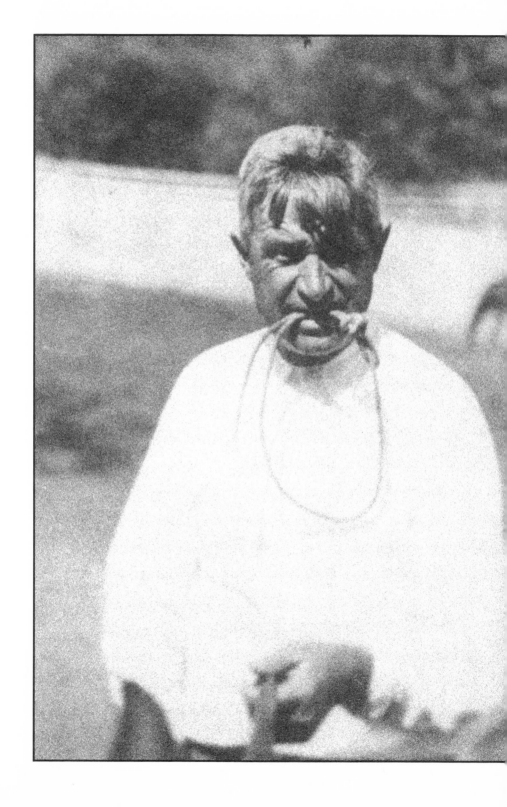

Desserts

Pumpkin Pie

1 (9 inch) unbaked pastry shell
2 Cups canned pumpkin
1 (14-ounce) can condensed milk (NOT EVAPORATED MILK)
2 eggs
2 Teaspoon salt
2 Teaspoon ground nutmeg
2 Teaspoon ground ginger
1 Teaspoon ground cinnamon

Pre-heat oven to 425°. In a large mixing bowl combine all ingredients, except the pastry shell. Mix well. Pour in pastry shell. Bake 15 minutes, reduce oven temperature to 350°. Continue baking 35 to 40 minutes or until knife inserted in middle of pie comes out clean.

Pie Crust

1-1/2 cups flour
1 Tablespoon sugar
1/2 Teaspoon salt
2/3 Cup Crisco
1/4 Cup water

Put 1 cup flour, sugar and salt into a bowl. Cut the Crisco into the flour. In a small bowl stir the 1/2 cup flour with the 1/4 cup water. Make a paste. Add the paste to the first mix, blend well. Form a ball with the dough. Roll out and place in a 9 inch pie pan.

Nancy Reid
State Park Ranger 1
Topanga State Park

Banana Cake

2-1/4 cups sugar
3/4 cup Wesson oil
3 eggs
2-1/2 cups flour
6 tablespoon buttermilk
1-1/2 teaspoons soda
4 large bananas (mashed)
1-1/2 teaspoons vanilla

Cream sugar, oil and egg yolks. Add bananas, buttermilk, and flour. Last, add egg whites (beaten stiff). Makes a big cake. Pour into greased pan and bake at 350 degrees for 35 to 45 minutes. GREAT!

Mrs. Clem (Donna) McSpadden
Chelsea, Oklahoma

Claremore, Okla., June 20. "Say, what do you know about Claremore having a golf course? I tell you turning your land into a golf course is the salvation of the farmer. That's the only thing to do with land now, is just to play golf on it."

Moose Meat Mince Meat

1 pound moose meat
1/2 pound beef suet
4 apples
1 quince
3/4 pound sugar
1/2 cup molasses
1 pint cider
1 pound seeded raisins
3/4 pound currants
1 tbls. finely cut citron
1/2 pint cooking brandy
1 tsp. cinnamon
1 tsp. mace
1 tsp. nutmeg
1 tsp. cloves
1/4 tsp. pepper
Salt to taste

Cover meat and suet with boiling water and cook until tender. Cool in water in which cooked. When cool remove layer of fat. Then finely chop meat and suet and add to it twice the amount of finely chopped apples, the quince finely chopped, sugar, molasses, cider, raisins, currants, and citron. Reduce stock in which meat and suet were cooked to 1-1/2 cups, and add to the fruit and meat mixture. Heat gradually, stirring occasionally, and cook slowly 2 hours (in thrift cooker). Add brandy and spices.

This can be put in jars while boiling hot and sealed for future use. This recipe makes 7 or 8 pints. Use as for any mince meat pie.

Governor Jay S. Hammond
State of Alaska

New Hampshire Wild Blueberry Pie

Spread over bottom of cooled, baked 9″ pie shell, 1 package of cream cheese (3 oz.) which has been softened. On top of this pour one pint of the largest and best blueberries, not cooked. Mash one pint of blueberries and add water, if necessary, to make 1-1/2 cups. Bring to a boil and gradually stir in mixture of 1 cup sugar and 3 Tblsp. of cornstarch. Cook over low heat, stirring constantly until boiling. Boil one minute. Cool. Pour over the berries in pie shell. Chill about 2 hours. Just before serving, decorate with whipped cream. Wild blueberries make the best pie, but cultivated berries may be used.

Governor Meldrim Thompson, Jr.
State of New Hampshire

"There is as many gadgets on the market to overhaul men as there is women. I doubt if women have got much on men when it comes to trying to outlook themselves."

Peach-Berry Cobbler

Serves 6 to 8
Bake at 375° for 40 to 45 minutes

Combine in sauce pan:
1/4 c. sugar
1/4 c. brown sugar
1 T. cornstarch
Add 1/2 c. water; blend well. Cook over medium heat, stirring constantly, until thick.

Add:
1 T lemon juice
2 cups slices peaches (4 medium)
1 cup blueberries. Turn into 2-quart baking dish.

COBBLER TOPPING
Sift together into mixing bowl
1 cup sifted flour
1/2 c. sugar
1-1/2 t. baking powder
1/2 t. salt

Add:
1/2 cup milk
1/4 cup soft butter, beat until smooth.

Spoon over fruit. Sprinkle with mixture of 2 T. sugar
and 1/4 t. nutmeg.

Harriet L. Axelrad
Docent, Will Rogers State Park

"I have always noticed that anytime a man can't come and settle with you without bringing his lawyer, why look out for him."

Pecan Pie

PIE FILLING
3 eggs slightly beaten
1 cup blue label Karo
1/8 t. salt
1 cup sugar
2/3 cup pecan meats
1 t. vanilla

Mix together all ingredients, adding nuts last. Pour into 9-inch pie plate lined with pie crust. Bake in 400° oven 10 minutes, then reduce to 325° and continue baking until a silver knife blade inserted in center of filling comes out clean.

Harriet L. Axelrad
Docent, Will Rogers State Park

"There is nothing as determined as a woman that carries on, and there is millions of 'em."

Maudie Dumas' Fresh Fruit Pie

(This came from a neighbor when I was a little girl. It's been a family favorite since the first bite.)

Ingredients:
1 baked pie shell
3 boxes of strawberries or,
6 to 8 peaches (use enough of either fruit to fill the crust)
1 C. sugar
3 T. cornstarch
1 C. whipping cream, whipped

Preparation:
Cut up and mash half of the fruit and cook with sugar and cornstarch until thick and clear. Cool. Just before serving, spoon half of cooked mixture into pie shell and spread to cover the bottom. Slice the rest of the fresh fruit and form a second layer in the shell. Top with final layer of cooked fruit, spreading it over all. Top with whipped cream. (To make it fancy, use a pastry bag to pipe the whipped cream on top.) Keep pie refrigerated until ready to cut and serve.

Carol Sandmeier
Volunteer, William S.Hart Ranch

"Presidents become great, but they have to make president first."

Scottish Scones

3 cups flour
1 tsp. baking soda
1 tsp. Cream of Tartar
1 tsp. sugar
a little salt
1/4 cup shortening
1 cup milk

Sift flour, soda, cream of tartar, sugar and salt. Break in shortening. Mix with milk to a soft dough. Pat dough to 1/2″ thick square. Cut into four, then cut each piece into four so you have triangular pieces. Bake 8 to 10 min. at 375 degrees.

Nancy Reid
State Park Ranger 1
Topanga State Park,

"A man that don't like a horse, there is something the matter with him."

Fresh Peach Ice Cream

6 eggs
2 cups sugar
1 Tablespoon Vanilla
pinch salt
1 Pint whipping cream
1-1/2 quart crushed fresh peaches
enough whole milk to fill the ice cream freezer to the proper level

Beat the eggs until light and fluffy. Add the sugar, salt and vanilla. Add cream and peaches. Mix well. This is better made the day before and refrigerate over night. Put the mix in the ice cream freezer. Fill to proper level. Follow directions of your ice crram freezer.

Don Raymond
Illustrator, Will Rogers Cookbook

"Art is when you do something just cockeyed from what is the right way to do it."

203

Caramel Custard

Custard:
4 egg yolks
1-1/2 cup milk
1/3 cup sugar
1 envelope plain gelatin (Soaked in 3 Tbls. cold water or milk.)
1 cup cream
1 teaspoon vanilla

Caramel:
2/3 cup sugar
2 teaspoons water

Make caramel and line pudding form. In top of double boiler mix egg yolks, milk and sugar. Cook over hot water until custard coats spoon. Add soaked gelatin, stir until disolved, add cream and vanilla. Cool, strain into caramel lined form and refrigerate until used.

Make dessert the evening before it is to be used, to give caramel lining a chance to melt.

Trudy Sandmeier

"I can always find the good in People, beyond that, I did not bother."

Grandma Zimmerman's Sour Cream Cookies

1 cup brown sugar
1/2 cup shortning
1 egg beaten
1/2 cup sour cream
1/2 tsp. salt
2 cups flour
1/2 tsp. nutmeg
1/2 tsp. baking soda
2 tsp. baking powder
1 cup chopped walnuts

Cream shortening and sugar together, add beaten egg and nuts. Sift together dry ingredients and add to mix, alternately with sour cream. Mix well and drop by teaspoon on greased baking sheet. Bake in pre-heated oven, at 400 degrees for 15 minutes.

Donna Raymond
Docent, Will Rogers State Park

"Where there is no malice in your heart there can be none shown in your home."

English Trifle

1 package yellow or pineapple layer cake mix (18.5 oz.)
1/2 cup raspberry jam
1/2 cup sherry or 1/3 cup orange juice, plus 2 tablespoons sherry flavoring
1 can vanilla ready-to-serve pudding (18 oz.) or make your own
1 cup chilled whipping cream
1/2 cup sugar
1/4 cup toasted slivered almonds
candied cherries, chopped

Bake cake in oblong pan, 13x9x2, as directed on package. Cool. Cut cake crosswise in half. Reserve one half for future use. Cut remaining half into 4 squares. Split each square, fill with 2 tablespoons jam. Arrange squares in 2 quart glass serving bowl, cutting squares to fit shape of bowl. Pour wine over cake and allow to soak into the cake a few minutes. Spread with pudding. Chill at least 8 hours. In chilled bowl, beat cream and sugar until stiff. Spread over trifle. Sprinkle with almonds and cherries.

Variation: Strawberry Trifle
Substitute 1 package frozen strawberry halves (16 ounces), thawed, for the raspberry jam. Omit sherry and do not fill cake squares. Arrange half the cake in bowl, top with half the strawberries and spread about 1/2 cup pudding over berries. Repeat. Chill at least 8 hours. In chilled bowl, beat cream and sugar until stiff, spread over trifle. Sprinkle with almonds and cherries. Serves 10 to 12.

Governor Robert F. Bennett
State of Kansas

Cranberry Crunch

1 cup quick cooking oatmeal
1/2 cup all purpose flour
1 cup brown sugar, firmly packed
1 stick margarine
1 (1 lb.) can whole cranberry sauce

Mix oatmeal, flour and brown sugar together. Cut in stick of margarine until mixture is crumbly. Pack 1/2 of this mixture into greased 8x8 pan. Cover with whole cranberry sauce. Top with remaining crumb mixture. Bake at 375 degrees for 45 minutes. Serve warm, topped with vanilla ice cream.

Governor James B. Longley
State of Maine

"You people certainly have a wonderful country in this America, . . ."

Carrot Pineapple Cake

2 cups grated carrots
2 cups sugar
1-1/2 cups vegetable oil
1 small can crushed pineapple, in juice.

Combine and beat ingredients; add 4 eggs, one at a time, beating well after each addition. Sift 2 cups flour with 2 teaspoons soda, 1 teaspoon salt, and 1 teaspoon cinnamon. Add to first mixture. Add 1 small can crushed pineapple, including juice. Bake in three eight inch layer pans greased, lined with waxed paper, then greased and floured. Bake in a pre-heated 350 degree oven about 35 minutes.

ICING
1 8-ounce package cream cheese
1 stick butter
Cream ingredients together and add 1 one-pound box powdered sugar, 1 teaspoon vanilla, and 1/2 cup nuts. Ice cake between layers only.

> Governor David L Boren
> State of Oklahoma

"Leaving the glorious State of Oklahoma tonight by popular demand."

Maggie Cake

1 cup butter
2-1/2 cups sugar
5 eggs, beaten separately
1 cup buttermilk
5 teaspoons coffee
2 teaspoons vanilla
3 cups flour
1 teaspoon baking powder
1 teaspoon soda
4 teaspoons cocoa
1 teaspoon salt

Mix ingredients. Add stiffly beaten egg whites last. Makes five layers.

ICING
1 pound powdered sugar
3 teaspoons coffee
1 egg
1/2 cup butter
2 teaspoons cocoa
1 teaspoon vanilla
dash of salt

Put all ingredients into mixing bowl except sugar. Start mixing, gradually adding sugar, and cream if needed, to make right consistency for spreading. Icing is good when chocked full of Oklahoma pecans.

This recipe is named for Mrs. Maggie Prather of Stratford, Oklahoma, who is a life-long friend of the A. H. Shi Family. The Shis are the parents of Mrs. Molly Shi Boren, First Lady of Oklahoma.

Governor David L. Boren
State of Oklahoma

Oma Cake

Ingredients:
1-1/2 cups sugar
3/4 cups shortening
2 1-oz squares chocolate
2 eggs
2 cups flour
1 tsp. baking soda
1 tsp. cinnamon
1 scant tsp. salt
1 cup buttermilk or sour milk
2 Tbsps. lemon juice

Cream sugar and shortening thoroughly. Add 1 egg, beat one minute. Add another egg, beat one minute. Melt 2 1-oz. chocolate squares and cool. Mix together flour, baking soda, cinnamon and salt. Mix alternately with milk. Add cool chocolate with lemon juice. Bake at 325 degrees for 25 minutes.

Filling:
2 egg yolks, 1/2 cup sugar, 1 tsp. vanilla, 1 cup milk, 3 tsp. flour,
Beat egg. Add sugar, flour. Add milk slowly – cook in double boiler until it thickens. Add vanilla.

Icing:
Beat 2 egg whites stiff. Add 3/4 cup confectioners sugar. In another bowl mix to smooth cream 1 cup confectioners sugar and 4 Tbsp. butter. Add 2 squares melted chocolate. Combine with stiff egg white and sugar. Mix and beat until nice, smooth, thick paste.

Oma Cake is one of the Governor's favorite recipes from his mother's collection.

Governor Richard A. Snelling
State of Vermont

Old Fashion Hot Fudge Sauce

1 cup cocoa
1 cup sugar
1/2 cup Carnation milk
1/2 cup water
1/2 pound marshmallows (small size)

Mix all ingredients except marshmallows. Let cook about one hour in top of double boiler. Add marshmallows, and let partly melt. Serve hot. You can cook in a microwave in a Pyrex container. Serves 8 - 10.

Mary Weiss
Docent, Will Rogers State Park

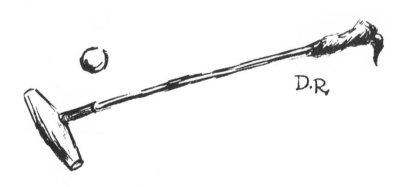

Virginia Apple Cake

1 cup salad oil
2 cups sugar
2 eggs (large)
3 cups chopped Virginia apples (tart)
2 t. vanilla
1/2 t. cinnamon
1/2 t. nutmeg
3 cups flour
1 t. baking soda
1 t. salt
1/2 cup chopped nuts (or 1 cup chopped pecans)
1/2 cup raisins
3 T. sugar mixed with 1 tsp. cinnamon for coating pan

Combine sugar and cinnamon mixture. Grease tube or bundt pan and shake sugar-cinnamon mixture around in it until sides and bottom are well coated.

Mix oil with sugar in electric mixer until well mixed. Add eggs one at a time beating well after each addition. Sift flour, cinnamon, nutmeg, baking soda and salt. Add vanilla and mix well. Slowly add the sifted flour mixture. Add the apples, nuts and raisins. Pour batter into pan and bake at 325 degrees for 1-1/2 to 2 hours. Usually 1-3/4 hours is about right. (Batter is unusually thick.)

Governor John N. Dalton
Commonwealth of Virginia

"Been traveling today down through the beautiful Shenandoah Valley of Virginia – and boobs are leaving to see Europe!"

Coconut Pound Cake

2 c. sugar
1 c. crisco
Cream together and add 5 eggs.
1 tsp. coconut flavoring
2 c. sifted flour
1-1/2 tsp. baking powder
1 c. buttermilk
1 tsp. salt
1 3-1/2 oz. package coconut

Mix all well together and put in a bundt pan. Bake one hour at 350 degrees.

Boil for one minute:
1 c. sugar
1/2 c. water
1 tsp. coconut flavoring

Pour over hot cake and let set 10 minutes, then remove from pan.

Ramona Wilt
President,
Pocahontas Womans Club
Claremore, Oklahoma

"Claremore, Okla. is just waiting for a high-tension line so they can go ahead with locating an airport."

Chocolate Buttermilk Cake

1/2 c butter, 1/2 c brown sugar, 1/2 c white sugar
2 eggs
2 squares chocolate, melted
1 tsp. vanilla
2 c. flour
1/2 tsp. salt
1/2 c. buttermilk
1 c. boiling water, with 1 tsp. soda in it.

Cream butter and sugars together, add eggs and beat, add melted chocolate and vanilla, beat until smooth. Add sifted ingredients and buttermilk alternately. Boil 1 C water and add 1 tsp. soda. Mix together. Bake at 350 degrees layer pan 30-35 min.; dripper pan, 40-45 min. Frost with chocolate frosting. This is a very moist cake.

Governor John V. Evans
State of Idaho

Norma Stouffer's Quick Lemon Crisps

2 cups all purpose flour
3/4 tsp. baking soda
Pinch of salt
3/4 cup shortening
1 cup sugar
2 packages lemon instant pudding
3 eggs, slightly beaten

Sift flour with baking soda and salt. Cream shortening, add sugar and pudding mix. Cream until light and fluffy. Add eggs, mix throughly, until well blended. Drop by teaspoon on a well greased baking sheet, about 2-1/2″ apart. Bake in 375 degree, pre-heated oven 8 to 10 minutes.

Donna Raymond
Docent, Will Rogers State Park

"A man that don't like love a horse, there is something the matter with him."

Molasses Cookies

1 Cup sugar
1 Cup molasses
4 Cups flour
1/2 Cup melted butter
1 Cup hot water
1 egg
1 Teaspoon salt
2 Teaspoons ground ginger
1 Teaspoon ground nutmeg
1 Teaspoon ground cloves
1 Teaspoon ground cinnamon
2 Teaspoons baking soda

Mix all ingredients together well and drop by teaspoon full on a cookie sheet. Bake 10 to 12 minutes. Bake in pre-heated 350° oven.

Michelle Gardner
State Park Ranger 1
Will Rogers State Park

Oatmeal Cake

Place in a bowl:
1-1/4 cup boiling water
1 cup quick oatmeal
1 stick oleo
Cover and let stand 20 minutes
Then add:
1 cup white sugar
1 cup brown sugar
2 eggs
1-1/2 cups sifted flour
1 teaspoon soda
1 teaspon cinnamon
1 teaspoon salt
Mix well and bake in oblong pan for 35 min. at 350 degrees.

TOPPING
2 tablespoons oleo
1/4 cup canned milk
1/2 cup sugar
1/2 cup coconut
1/2 cups chopped nuts
1/2 teaspoon vanilla

Mix in sauce pan till sugar is melted. Spread over hot cake and place under broiler until bubbly and slightly browned.

Will Rogers made his first radio broadcast over Pittsburgh's pioneer radio station KDKA in 1922.

Governor Milton J. Sharp
State of Pennsylvania

Wine Cake

1 package yellow cake mix
1 package vanilla instant pudding
4 eggs
1 tsp. nutmeg
3/4 cup oil
3/4 cup cream sherry

Mix ingredients together for 5 minutes. Pour into a greased and floured angel food cake pan (removable center type). Bake at 350 degrees for 50 minutes. When cooled, turn cake out of pan. Top with whipped cream when served, if you wish.

A sauce to pour over whipped cream may be made by creaming any type of canned fruit in a blender. A small amount of brandy may be added to the fruit if desired.

This cake is excellent for picnics, since it does not need a topping and may be preserved by wrapping in foil.

Governor Mike O'Callaghan
State of Nevada

Carrot Cake

2 cups sugar
1 cup salad oil (I use corn oil)
4 eggs
1 teaspoon vanilla
Beat well. Add slowly to mixture of dry ingredients:
2 cups plain flour
2 teaspoons baking powder
1/2 teaspoon salt
2 teaspoons soda
2 teaspoons cinnamon

Fold in 3 cups of grated carrots. Bake in three well greased and lined 8 inch pans for 25 minutes at 350 degrees.

Filling:
1 stick corn oil margarine,
8 ounce package of cream cheese
1 box powdered sugar
1 cup chopped nuts
1 teaspoon vanilla

Let ingredients stand at room temperature before mixing. Mix and spread between layers and on top.

Governor James B. Hunt, Jr.
State of North Carolina

Wonder Cookies

1 cup peanut butter
1 cup pitted and chopped dates
1 cup chopped nuts
1 can Eagle brand condensed milk

Mix well and drop from spoon on cookie sheet and bake slowly.

Mary Pickford

Banana Bread

1/2 cup butter
1 cup sugar
2 eggs
3 bananas (not to ripe)
1/2 tsp. vanilla
2 cups flour
Pinch salt
1 cup finely chopped nuts

Mix as for a cake, cream butter, and sugar, beat eggs. Sift dry ingredients. Beat into mixture alternating with mashed bananas. Add nuts. Bake in a loaf pan for 50 minutes, in a preheated oven. (350 degrees)

Harriet L. Axelrad
Docent, Will Rogers State Park

"I have always noticed that anytime a man can't come and settle with you without bringing his lawyer, why look out for him."

Sugar Surprises

3/4 cup butter
2 cups brown sugar
2 eggs beaten
1 cup flour
1 teaspoon vanilla
3/4 cup nut meats
1 teaspoon baking powder

Cream butter and sugar, add other ingredients in order given. Pour into a 10 x 14 inch pan about 1 inch deep. Bake 20 to 30 minutes in a moderate oven. The batter will rise and then fall – the secret is to take out as soon as it falls. Cut into any size squares or fingers that you like.

James B. Edwards
Governor – State of South Carolina

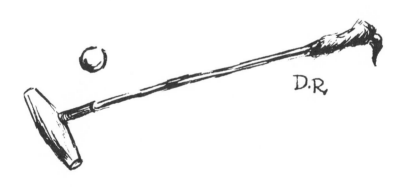

Ranger Cookies

1 cup butter
1 cup granulated sugar
1 cup brown sugar, packed
2 eggs, well beaten
2 cups sifted flour
1/2 teaspoon baking powder
1/2 teaspoon salt
1 teaspoon baking soda
1 teaspoon vanilla
2 cups oats
2 cups cornflakes*
1/2 cup coconut
1/2 cup chopped walnuts*

Cream butter with sugars until light and fluffy. Beat in eggs. Sift flour with baking powder, salt and soda. Blend into creamed mixture. Add vanilla, cereals, coconut and nuts. Mix until blended.

Drop dough by 2-1/2 tablespoons or by ice cream scoop (No. 24) onto ungreased baking sheet. Flatten to 4-inch diameter.

Bake at 350 degrees 10 to 12 minutes. Cookies should be slightly soft when removed from oven. Makes about 22 large.

Note: For small cookies, use rounded teaspoon dough, do not flatten and bake at 375 degrees 8 to 10 minutes. Makes about 6 dozen.

*Rice crispies and chopped almonds are great substitutes for the cornflakes and walnuts.

Barbara Rodriguez
Office Assistant #2
Will Rogers State Park

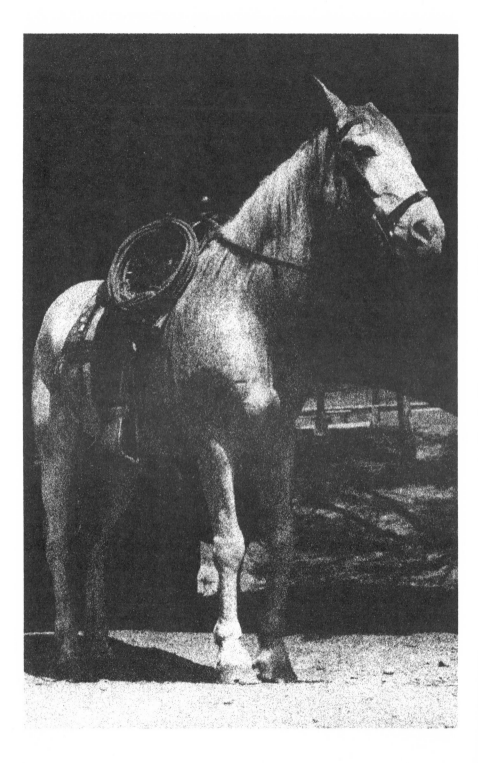

Lemon Squares

1 cup Gold Medal flour
1/2 cup butter or margarine, softened
1/4 cup confectioners sugar
2 eggs
1 cup granulated sugar
1/2 tsp. baking powder
1/4 tsp. salt
2 tbsp. lemon juice

Heat oven to 350 degrees. Cream flour, butter and confectioners sugar. Press evenly in bottom of ungreased square pan, 9x9x2 or 8x8x2. Bake 20 minutes. Beat remaining ingredients until light and fluffy, about 3 minutes. Pour over hot crust and bake about 25 minutes longer or until no imprint remains when touched lightly in center. Cool and cut into 2″ squares. Makes 16.

Chocolate Squares
Follow recipe for Lemon Squares except – decrease butter to 1/3 cup, omit lemon juice, and add 1 sq. (1oz.) unsweetened chocolate, melted and cooled, to beaten egg mixture.

Governor Milton J. Shapp
State of Pennsylvania

Betty's Cherry Nut Cake

2 sticks butter or oleo
2 c. sugar
2 c. flour
4 egg yolks
1 t. vanilla
1 c. chopped pecans
1 small bottle maraschino cherries, cut and drained
4 egg whites, beaten

Mix all ingredients except egg whites. Fold beaten egg whites in. Bake in greased angel food pan at 325 degrees for one hour, ten minutes. Cool in pan. Freezes well. This may also be baked in the small cake tins (2-1/2 x 5 inches). It will make five of these.

Gene Asanovich
Docent, Will Rogers State Park

Fudgey Brownies

1/2 cup butter or oleo
4 sq. unsweetened chocolate
4 eggs
2 c. sugar
1 c sifted flour
1 tsp. vanilla
1 c. chopped nuts

Melt butter and chocolate over hot water; cool slightly. Beat eggs until foamy. Gradually add sugar, beating well after each addition. Add chocolate mixture and blend. Stir in flour, add vanilla and nuts. Spread in a greased and floured 9x9x2 inch pan. Bake at 325 degrees for 40 minutes; cool and cut in squares.

Ramona Henry Wilt
President of the Pocahontas Womans
Club of Claremore, Oklahoma

Will was a member of the Womens Club for a summer. He and a few of his boyfriends went in on a dare. Will was made an Honorary member. The club was organized on June 29, 1899.

Spider Cookies

1 12 oz. pkg. Butterscotch Bits
1 12 oz. pkg. Nestles Chocolate chips
1 c cocktail nuts
1 large pkg. Chinese Noodles

Melt Butterscotch Bits in double boiler, then melt chocolate chips. Add nuts and noodles. Mix well. Drop by spoonful onto waxpaper. Refrigerate 1/2 hour only. Makes 48 cookies.

Mary Olivera
Docent, Will Rogers State Park

228

Hummingbird Cake A'la Richard

3 cups all-purpose flour
2 cups sugar
1 teaspoon baking soda
1/2 teaspoon salt
1 teaspoon ground cinnamon
3 eggs beaten well
1 cup vegetable oil
1-1/2 teaspoons vanilla
1 8 ounce can crushed pineapple
1 cup chopped nuts
2 cups chopped bananas

Combine first five ingredients in a large bowl, blend well. Add eggs and oil, stirring until dry ingredients are moistened, do not beat. Stir in the vanilla, pineapple, bananas, nuts.

Spread into a greased 13 x 11 Pyrex. Bake at 350 degrees for 30-40 minutes. (Check with toothpick.) Cool before Icing.

Cream Cheese Frosting
1 8 ounce package cream cheese, softened
1 16 ounce package powdered sugar (3-1/2 to 4 cups)
1/2 cup softened butter
1 teaspoon vanilla

Combine cream cheese and butter. Beat until smooth. Add sugar and vanilla, beat until light and fluffy. Be sure the cake is cold before it is frosted.

Donna Raymond
Docent, Will Rogers State Park

"The Lord so constituded everybody that no matter what color you are you require about the same amount of nourishment."

Pots De Creme De Chocolat

1 Cup semi-sweet chocolate chips
1 1/4 Cup scalded light coffee cream
2 Egg yolks
3 T Grand Marnier brandy, rum or Creme de Menthe

Scald cream. Add it and all other ingredients to blender container. Turn blender on high speed until chocolate chips are well blended. Pour into individual pots de creme, or demi-tasse cups. Chill well, at least 6 hours.

Serves 8

Colonel Robert and Eloise Gleason.

On August 16th, 1935, with weather conditions just as treacherous as on the preceding day, Robert Gleason, as radio operator, dared with pilot Joe Crosson to fly to Barrow, Alaska, to bring back the bodies of Will Rogers and Wiley Post to Fairbanks, Seattle and finally to Los Angeles.

"You know, this radio has made it mighty fine to find out what's ahead. You see, it's never the weather you take off in, it's the weather where you have to go through after you take off. I remember one trip on our late tour with Captain Frank Hawks when we took off one day in a snow storm in New Mexico, when you just couldn't see a thing, not two hundred feet, and it was that way flying blind for the next hour, but he had heard before that it was clear in Albuquerque, where we were going. So it's how is the weather ahead of you, [rather] than how is it where you are."

"Oklahoma Crude" Cake

2 Sticks of margarine
1/2 Cup water
4 Tbsp. cocoa
2 Cups flour, sifted
2 Cups sugar
1 Cup buttermilk
2 Eggs, beaten
1 tsp. soda
1/4 tsp. salt

Heat together margarine, water and cocoa, stirring constantly until margarine is melted. Pour over flour and sugar; add eggs, soda, buttermilk and salt. Bake in greased jelly roll pan at 350 degrees for 25 minutes. Frost while warm.

Frosting
1 Stick margarine
4 Tbsp. cocoa
6 Tbsp. milk
1 lb Pkg powdered sugar
1 tsp. vanilla
1 Cup nuts, chopped

About five minutes before cake is done, melt margarine, cocoa and milk, stirring constantly. Pour this mixture over powdered sugar, vanilla and nuts. Mix well and frost warm cake. Variation: 1 tsp. cinnamon may be added to cake frosting.

Max Weitzenhoffer
Co-producer of
The Will Rogers Follies

"There was a Moral Crusade on in New York City, but it only lasted two days. They appointed a jury to investigate all the soiled plays. . . Our show, the Follies, is so tame it is listed in the Amusement columns with the churches."

231

Apple Cake

2 cups Flour
1 tsp. Baking Powder
1 tsp. Salt
1 tsp. Cinnimon
2 cups Chopped Nuts
4 cups Chopped Apples
2 Eggs
2 cups Sugar
1/2 cup oil
1 tsp. Vanilla

Pre-heat oven to 350°. In a large bowl, mix together dry ingredients. Then add the rest. Grease a 9x13 baking pan. Spread batter in the pan. (It will be thick.) Bake until golden brown, approximately one hour.

Lorraine Bothwell
Docent, Will Rogers State Park

Pots de Creme

6 oz. chocolate chips
3/4 c. milk
1 egg
1/4 c. sugar
1 tsp. vanilla
dash of salt

Put chocolate chips, egg, sugar and salt into a blender. Heat the milk just to boiling and pour into the blender. Blend for 30 seconds, till all the chips are melted. Add the vanilla and 1/2 tblsp. of brandy or other liquor, if desired. Pour into small cups and refrigerate till firm. You may decorate them with nuts, whipped cream, shaved chocolate or a cherry.

Governor Richard D. Lamm
State of Colorado

Favorite Ice Cream

One quart buttermilk
One pint whipping cream
Two cups sugar
One tablespoon vanilla

Mix all ingredients and pour into ice cream churn and freeze.

This is Gov. Edwards' grandmother's recipe.

Governor James B. Edwards
State of South Carolina

Southern Red Velvet Cake

1/2 c. shortening
1-1/2 c. sugar
2 eggs
2 c. all-purpose flour (sift 3 or 4 times)
1 t. baking soda
1 t. vinegar
1 rounded t. cocoa (optional)
1/2 t. salt
1 tsp. vanilla
2 oz. red food coloring
1 cup buttermilk

Cream shortening and sugar. Add eggs, beat well. Alternately add dry ingredients (flour, cocoa, and salt) and buttermilk. Add vanilla and coloring. Dissolve soda in vinegar, add to batter. Bake in 2 eight inch layer pans or a 9x13 pan at 350 degrees for 25-35 minutes.

Frosting and filling:
1/2 c. flour
1 stick oleo
dash salt
1 c. sugar
1 c. milk
1 t.vanilla
1/2 c. shortening
2 c. coconut

Cook flour, salt, and milk over low heat until in soft pudding stage. Set aside to cool. Cream shortenings, sugar, and vanilla. Add to cooled pudding. Spread between layers and over lake. Sprinkle with coconut. This is a very moist. cake and keeps for days. It is really a pretty red color.

Gene Asanovich
Docent, Will Rogers State Park

"We elect our Presidents, be they Republican or Democrat, then start daring 'em to make good."

Chocolate Ice Box Dessert

Ingredients:
chocolate chips
sugar
water
eggs
whipping cream
vanilla
salt
angelfood cake

Method:
Line flat 9x9 cake pan with wax paper. Slice angelfood cake and place a layer of cake in cake pan. (I find that angelfood cake slices better if frozen.) Separate six (6) eggs, beat egg yolks. Melt one (1) twelve ounce package of chocolate chips in a double boiler or over water, when melted add four (4) tablespoons of sugar and six (6) tablespoons of tap water, mix well, be sure sugar melts.

Remove from heat and stir the above hot chocolate mixture gradually into the beaten yolks of eggs, beat until smooth. Cool chocolate mixture. Add two (2) teaspoons of vanilla and one teaspoon salt, mix. Beat the six (6) egg whites until stiff; whip two (2) cups of whipping cream. Fold egg whites into the cooled chocolate mixture, then the whipping cream. Place a layer of the chocolate mixture on the sliced angelfood cake, then another layer of cake, then a layer of chocolate. Place in refrigerator and chill overnight. This may be frozen and used later. Be sure to chill overnight before freezing.

Gerald R. Ford

President and Mrs. Gerald R. Ford

"Mertz" Poor Man's Cake

1 cup brown sugar
1/3 cup lard or Crisco
1 teaspoon cinnamon
1/2 teaspoon cloves
1/4 teaspoon nutmeg
1 teaspoon soda
1/2 teaspoon salt
2 cups seedless raisins
1 cup water
1/2 teaspoon baking powder
2 cups flour

Put all the ingredients, except flour, baking powder and soda, in a saucepan. Bring to a boil, and boil three minutes. Cool completely This may take an hour. Sift together dry ingredients. Mix in to the cooled mix, beat for three minutes.

Pour into a greased 9x9 pan. Bake in a 350 degree oven for 45 minutes.

Serves eight, keeps moist a week or more. Adding walnuts is optional. Good for Holiday Gifts.

Ethel Haydon
Docent, Will Rogers State Park

"If your time is worth anything travel by air, if not you might just as well walk."

Lemon Squares

1-1/2 cups flour
3/4 cup of butter
Cut butter into flour like pie crust. Pat down in baking pan, (9x11).
Bake 10 minutes at 350 degrees till light brown.

Filling:
1 cup brown sugar
1-1/2 cups coconut (shredded)
1 cup chopped nuts
2 eggs beaten
1/4 tsp. baking powder
1/2 tsp. vanilla

Mix together and spread on above crust. Bake 20 minutes, 350
degrees until light brown. Let cool, then ice with:

Icing:
1 cup powdered sugar
1 tblsp butter (melted)
Juice and rind (grated) of one lemon
Cream together and spread over the above. Cut in 2 inch squares.

Nelda Lockwood
Park Aide, Will Rogers State Park

237

F.R.F.'S Southern Delight

1 Box cake mix (White or Yellow)
1 Large can crushed pineapple
1 Family size instant Vanilla Pudding mix
1 Large cool whip
1 cup chopped walnuts or Pecans

Bake cake as per directions on the box, in a 9x13 pan. While cake cools drain pineapple. (Leave a small amount of syrup for moisture.) Set aside. Mix and set aside pudding mix. When cake is cold, spread pineapple over cake, spread pudding over pineapple. Spread large container of cool whip over pudding. Top with nuts. Keep in refrigerator until ready to use. ENJOY!!!

Don Raymond
Illustrator, Will Rogers Cookbook

"What constitutes a life well spent? Love and admiration from your fellow men is all anyone can ask."

238

Pumpkin Cake

Box Spiced cake mix
1 cup chopped nuts
1 cube melted butter
1 large can pumpkin
1 cup sugar
4 eggs
1 tsp. ground ginger
1 tsp. cinnamon
1/2 tsp. ground cloves

Mix pumpkin, milk, eggs, ginger, cinnamon, and cloves well. Pour in a 9x13 pan or Pyrex dish. Sprinkle with dry spice cake mix (over Filling). Sprinkle with chopped nuts. Dribble melted butter over top. Bake for one hour and fifteen minutes at 350 degrees. (Until custard is set.)

Etta Lou Rose
Docent, Will Rogers State Park

"We are the first nation in the history of the world to go to the poorhouse in an automobile."

Rodgers Dodger's Dutch Baby

One cup flour
One cup milk
Four eggs
Half stick (4 tbs.) butter or margerine

Preheat Oven to 425 degrees
Place the butter in a cast iron frying pan and let it melt in the oven until the butter starts to sizzle. (You can use less butter if you wish.)

Blend eggs, milk and flour in a blender, alternating the milk and flour. Once butter has started to sizzle (bubble) add the mixture to the frying pan.

Bake for twenty to thirty minutes or until the top is a golden brown and a toothpick comes out of the center clean.

Serve with Powder sugar and/or lemon juice.

Feeds two people.

Michelle Gardner
State Park Ranger 1

"You can't beat an administration by attacking it, you have to show some plan of improving it."

Walnut Meringues

2 egg whites
1-1/2 teaspoons vanilla
1/4 teaspoon salt
2/3 cup sugar
2 teaspoons grated orange peel
2 cups walnuts, cut in pieces

Preheat oven to 250 degrees. Combine egg whites, vanilla and salt. Beat with electric beater until foamy. Add sugar a tablespoon at a time, beating after each addition. Beat till soft peaks form and all sugar is dissolved. Fold in orange peel and walnuts.

Drop rounded teaspoons on cooky sheet covered with baking paper. Top with more walnuts, if desired.

Bake at 250 degrees till dry and a very light ivory color. Turn off oven and leave in 1 hour longer. Makes about 4 dozen cookies.

Ranger Gary McLaughlin
Will Rogers State Park

"No one is going to spoil the country but the people. No one man can do it and all the people are not going to do it, so its going to run in spite of all the mistakes that can happen to it."

Cafe's Pecan Pumpkin Pie and Carmel Sauce

1 29-ounce can pumpkin pie mix
1 5-ounce can evaporated milk
3 eggs, lightly beaten
1 cup sugar
1/2 teaspoons salt
2 teaspoons cinnamon
1 package yellow cake mix with pudding
1/2 pound butter, melted and cooled slightly
1-1/2 cup chopped pecans

Preheat oven to 350°. Line two 9 inch pie pans with waxed paper. Mix together the pumpkin, milk, sugar, eggs, salt and cinnamon. Pour into pans. Sprinkle cake mix over the top. Distribute chopped pecans over cake mix and drizzle melted butter over all. Bake 1 hour. Chill. Invert and cut into wedges. Thin wedges can be eaten with the fingers. Large wedges can be served on a plate, topped with a dollop of whipped cream, and warm carmel sauce drizzled over the top. This is a delicious alternative to pumpkin pie and extremely easy top make. Do not be thrown off by the use of the packaged cake mix.

Carmel Sauce (2 cups)
2 sticks (or 1 cup) sweet butter
2 cups light brown sugar
1 cup heavy cream

Cut butter into pieces and melt in a small heavy-bottomed pan. Stir in the brown sugar and cream. Cook over very low heat, stirring constantly, until all is melted and blended. Whisking the sauce helps to bring it together. Serve warm, Refrigerate what is not used. Reheat on low heat.

Whipped Cream
2 cups heavy whipping cream
3 tablespoons powdered sugar
1-1/2 teaspoon vanilla

Whip cream in a medium bowl, add sugar and vanilla any time after you first start whipping. Whip into soft peaks. Refrigerate till ready to use.

Dorothy and Irv Gordon
Docent, Will Rogers State Park

Walnut Torte

8 eggs, seperated
1 cup powdered sugar, sifted
1 cup ground walnuts
1 teaspoon flour
1 teaspoon ground coffee
1 teaspoon vanilla

Beat 8 egg yolks, add sugar and beat. Add vanilla, walnuts, flour and coffee. Beat egg whites stiff, fold into the mix. Bake in two layers about 20 minutes in a 375° oven (pre-heated.) Fill with chocolate mousse.

Chocolate Moose

1 package Bakers German Sweet chocolate
3 Tablespoons sugar
2 Tablespoons water
4 egg yolks
2 pint whipping cream (stiff)

Melt chocolate, sugar, and water in microwave oven. Add egg yolks, one at a time, cool. Add whipped cream a little at a time. Put between layers and on top of torte.

Mary Weiss
Docent, Will Rogers State Park

Heaven

1 cup flour
1 stick butter
3 oz. chopped pecans
1 8 oz. cream cheese
1 cup powdered sugar
1 cup whipping cream-use cool whip. Buy the largest container of cool whip
1 4oz. (small) choc. fudge instant pudding
1 4 oz. (small) vanilla instant pudding
3 cups cold milk

First layer: 9x11 glass pan

Blend flour and butter. Add pecans, pat into the bottom of the pan. Bake 350 degrees for 20 minutes.

Second layer:
Blend (use beater): cream cheese, powdered sugar, 1 cup cool whip pour over cooled crust

Third layer:
Blend (use beater) both puddings and milk. Pour over cream cheese layer.

Fourth layer:
Frost with the remaining cool whip. Shave chocolate over top.

Dorothy and Irv Gordan
Docent, Will Rogers State Park

Lorie's Grasshopper Dessert

Beat 1/2 pint whipping cream until stiff. Blend in 1 pint soft vanilla ice cream. Add 2 T green cream de menthe, and 2 T white cream de cacao. Add a few drops green food color. Pour into sherbert glasses. Freeze until firm.

Variations:
Pink Squirrel
Substitute 1/4 cup cream de cacao and 1/2 t almond flavoring for cream de menthe and cream de cacao in grasshopper recipe. Add a few drops red food coloring instead of green.

Brandy Alexander
Substitute 2 T Brandy and 2 T cream de cacao for cream de menthe and cream de cacao in grasshopper recipe.

John Falk
State Park Ranger

"I never saw an audience that I ever faced with any confidence."

Hasty Cake

Sift together:
1 cup sugar
1 cup flour
1/2 tsp. salt
1 tsp. baking powder

Melt in a measuring cup about 1/3 cup butter. When cool drop in one large or two small eggs and fill cup up with milk.

Add one teaspoon vanilla and mix *well* the dry and liquid ingreidents. Bake in about 400 degree oven until the cake springs back when touched with finger, about 20 minutes.

BUBBLE CAKE
Spread the following topping over the hasty cake when you take it from the oven, and then put it under the broiler very briefly until it begins to bubble and brown lightly.

To 1 cup brown sugar add about 1 teaspoon of flour, some broken nut meats, some coconut if you have it, vanilla and cream enough to make it spread easily.

I am happy to offer the following, which was a favorite of my grandmother's and is much admired by all her descendants.

Robert Abernethy
1972 – Citizen of the Year
Pacific Palisades
NBC Television – Washington, D.C.

Ozark Pudding

1 egg and 3/4 cup of sugar, beaten for a long time until very smooth.
Add to egg-sugar mixture: 2 tablespoons of flour, 1-1/2 teaspoon
baking powder, and 1/4 teaspoon salt.
Fold in: 1/2 cup of chopped raw apple
1/3 cup of chopped nut meats
1 teaspoon vanilla

Bake at 350 degrees in a well greased pie plate for 30 to 35 minutes.
Serve with whipped cream or ice cream. A little rum adds to the
taste.

Apparently this will fall, but that is correct.

Bess Truman

Mrs. Harry S. (Bess) Truman

Peach Ice Cream

Make a boiled custard of 1 quart cream, 1 pint milk, 3 eggs, 1 cup
sugar. To this, when cool, add 1/2 gallon of soft peaches mashed and
well sweetened. This makes one gallon of ice cream which is most
delicious.

With our Stonewall peaches this makes our very favorite "company
dessert" – a summer treat without equal.

Mrs. Lyndon B. Johnson

Lady Bird Johnson

Dodi's Whoopie Pies

2 cups granulated sugar
2 teaspoons vanilla
1 cup shortening
4 cups sifted flour
2 eggs
1 cup cocoa
1 cup sour milk (1 tablespoon vinegar or lemon juice plus sweet milk to make 1 cup)
2 teaspoons salt
2 teaspoons soda
1 cup hot water

FILLING
2 egg whites
4 tablespoons milk
2 teaspoons vanilla
2 cups powdered sugar
4 tablespoons flour
1 1/2 cups shortening

Cream sugar and shortening. Add eggs and beat until creamy. Add sour milk and vanilla. Sift flour, cocoa and salt and add to mixture. Dissolve soda in hot water and add. Drop by teaspoonsful on cookie sheet and bake at 400 degrees for 8-10 minutes. When cookies are cool, put them together in pairs with a generous dollop of filling. To make filling: beat egg whites; add vanilla, flour, milk and sugar. Beat together and mix well with shortening.

Randy Young
Docent, Will Rogers State Park
1991 Citizen of the Year
Pacific Palisades

Aunt Freda's Peanut Butter Cookies

2 cups flour
3/4 tsp. baking soda
1/2 tsp. baking powder
1/4 tsp. salt
1/2 cup butter
1/2 cup peanut butter
1/2 cup brown sugar
1/2 cup granulated sugar
1 egg
1/4 cup orange juice

Mix all well together. Roll in balls, the size of a walnut. Put on a lightly greased cookie sheet. Press ball down with a fork dipped in granulated sugar. Bake in 350 degree oven 10 to 12 minutes. Cookie is soft and keeps well.

Donna Raymond
Docent, Will Rogers State Park

"Be a politician; no training necessary."

Plum Pudding

1 quart seeded raisins
1 pint currants
1 pint finely cut citron
1 quart finely cut apples
1 quart finely cut suet
1 heaping quart bread crumbs
1 quart juice (grape etc.)
8 beaten eggs
1 pint sugar
nutmeg, cinnamon, spices to taste

Method:
Enough flour to make a stiff dough added to the above as given.
Steam four hours. This makes four nice puddings. Reheat by
steaming one when wanted, and serve with hard sauce made as
follows: Cream 1/2 pound of butter, gradually adding 3/4 pound
powdered sugar, stirring and beating until like whipped cream.
Flavor with vanilla and nutmeg.

Sallie Rogers McSpadden
(sister of Will Rogers)
Chelsea, Oklahoma

Will lived with his sister Sallie and her husband Tom McSpadden when
he went to the Drumgoole School.

Old Fashioned Sugar Cookies

2-3/4 Cups sifted flour
2 teaspoons baking powder
1/2 teaspoon salt
1/2 Cup butter or shortening
1 Cup sugar
2 eggs, well beaten
1 teaspoon vanilla

Sift flour once, measure, add baking powder and salt, and sift again. Cream butter thoroughly, add sugar gradually, and cream together until light and fluffy. Add eggs and beat well. Add vanilla. Add flour and blend. Chill 10 to 15 minutes. Roll 1/8 inch thick on slightly floured board. Cut with large floured cutter, and sprinkle with sugar. Place on ungreased baking sheet and bake in hot oven (400 degrees-10 to 12 minutes). Makes 2-1/2 dozen 3-1/2 inch cookies. For holidays, sprinkle with red or green sugar, colored candies, or decorate as desired.

Karen Sue Sapp
Docent, Will Rogers State Park

"Just flew in from Santa Barbara and found a real, legitimate use for my polo field. We landed on it."

Oldtime Cinnamon Jumbles

Mix thoroughly . . .
1/2 cup shortening
1 cup sugar
1 egg

Stir in . . .
3/4 cup buttermilk
1 tsp. vanilla

Sift together and stir in . . .
2 cups flour
1/2 tsp. soda
1/2 tsp. salt

Chill dough. Drop rounded teaspoonfuls about 2″ apart on lightly greased baking sheet. Sprinkle with mixture of sugar and cinnamon (1/4 cup sugar and 1 tsp. cinnamon). Bake until set but not brown.
Tempeature: 400 degrees
Time: Bake 8 to 10 min.
Amount: About 4 dozen 2″ cookies

Governor Scott M. Matheson
State of Utah

Carrot Pudding

1 cup grated carrots
1 cup grated potato
1 cup chopped suet
1 cup brown sugar
1-1/2 cups flour
1 tsp. soda dissolved in hot water
2 tsp. cinnamon
1 tsp. salt
2 cups seedless raisins

Mix all ingredients together and put into greased molds – fill two-thirds full and cover with waxed paper. Steam well for 2 hours. Serve with butter sauce.

BUTTER SAUCE
1 cup sugar
1 egg
1/2 cup butter
Juice and grated rind of one lemon
1 tsp. ground nutmeg
1 cup boiling water

Beat egg slightly with a fork, add other ingredients except water. Pour boiling water in slowly, stirring while you do so. Keep sauce hot, but do not boil.

Governor Meldrim Thomson
State of New Hampshire

Centennial Luncheon Apple Crisp

4 c. sliced apples
1 tsp. cinnamon
1 tsp. salt
1/4 c. water
Mix together the above ingredients.
3/4 c. sifted flour
1 c sugar
1/3 c. butter

Rub the three above ingredients together. Drop mixture over apples.
Bake. Serve warm with Whipped Cream. Use a buttered 10x6x2″
Baking Dish.
Temperature - 350 degrees
Time - 40 minutes
Amount - 6 servings

Betty Blake Rogers, Will's wife

"The day I roped Betty, I did the star performance of my life."

Nutty Fudge Pie

3/4 c. pecans
2 T. cooking oil
Roast pecans 350 degrees for 15-30 minutes. Toss now and then.
Drain on paper towel. Salt.

Fudge Sauce:
1 c. chocolate chips
1 c. small marshmallows
1 c. Pet milk
Salt

Cook over medium heat until thick. Stir to prevent sticking. Cool.
Line pie tin and sides with vanilla wafers. Fill half of tin with
vanilla ice cream. Pour 1/2 fudge sauce over ice cream. Fill with ice
cream and press into pan. Top with remaining fudge sauce. Sprinkle
top with pecans. Freeze. Serves 8.

Gov. Robert D. Ray
Iowa

Coffee Ice Cream

Serves 8
6 egg yolks, beaten
3/4 cup sugar
4-1/2 pints whipping cream
4 tablespoons instant Sanka coffee
1 tablespoon Vanilla extract
1/2 cup Cognac

Combine whipping cream, sugar, coffee and vanilla. Heat until it begins to simmer and then pour over egg yolks. Stir well and strain. Allow mixture to chill, stirring from time to time, until completely cold. Add cognac.

This recipe is one that was enjoyed by Mr. and Mrs. Louis B. Mayer, and was given by their daughter, Mrs. William Goetz.

Chocolate Nut Bars

2/3 c. shortening
1 pkg. brown sugar
3 eggs
1 t. vanilla
2 c. flour
1 t. baking powder
1/2 t. salt
1 c. walnuts
1-7 oz. pkg. chocolate chips

Cream shortening, sugar, eggs, and vanilla. Add sifted dry ingredients, nuts and chocolate chips. Pour into a well-greased 10-1/2 x 15-1/2″ pan or a pizza pan with a 14″ diameter. Bake at 350° for 25 minutes.

Gail and David Sears
District Interpretive Specialist
State of California

256

Strawberry Roll Supreme

6 eggs, separated
1/4 teaspoon cream of tartar
1 cup granulated sugar
1 teaspoon grated lemon rind
2 tablespoons lemon juice
1/4 teaspoon salt
1 cup sifted cake flour
2 cups heavy cream
2 tablespoons sugar
1/2 teaspoon vanilla
2-1/2 cups strawberries
2 tablespoons sugar

Beat egg whites until foamy. Add cream of tartar, beating until stiff. Gradually (1 tablespoon at a time) beat in 1/2 cup of sugar. Beat egg yolks until thick and lemon-colored. Beat 1/2 cup of sugar, lemon rind, and lemon juice. Gently fold egg-yolk mixture into egg white mixture. Sift flour with salt. Fold into egg mixture, gradually. Pour into foil-lined pan (15x10x1) . Bake in pre-heated oven (375 degrees) for 18 to 20 minutes. When baked, turn out on towel that has been sprinkled with confectioners sugar. Remove foil from cake immediately. Roll up cake in the towel from the 10 inch end and let stand until cold.

Whip heavy cream adding 2 tablespoons sugar and vanilla.

Sprinkle sliced strawberries with 2 tablespoons sugar and allow to stand about five minutes. Reserve several perfect strawberries, slicing in half, to garnish top of cake roll.

Unroll cake carefully and spread with half cup of whipped cream and sugared strawberries. Roll the cake and frost with remaining whipped cream. Garnish with the halved strawberries.

Robert K. Dornan
Congressman – 27th District
California

Banana Split Cake

1 stick margarine
1/2 cup sugar
2 cups graham cracker crumbs

Mix and press into 13x 9 Pyrex dish.
2 sticks margarine
2 eggs
2 cups confectioners sugar

Mix in electric mixer for 15 minutes, yes, 15 minutes. Pour over crumb mixture. Drain large can of pineapple chunks and layer over margarine, sugar and egg mixture. Slice enough bananas to make a generous layer over pineapple chunks. Cover with large container of Cool-Whip frozen dessert topping. Garnish with cherries and pecans and chill overnight. (Several hours will be satisfactory, if it is not possible to chill overnight.) Serves 9 to 12, depending on size of servings.

Cliff French
Governor, Mississippi

Pistachio Pie

Combine in small mixing bowl
2/3 cup sugar
1/4 cup water
1 unbeaten egg white
9 drops green food coloring
1 teaspoon lemon juice
1 teaspoon almond extract

Beat with electric mixer at highest speed until soft peaks form when beaters are raised, 3 to 5 minutes.

Beat 1 cup whipping cream until thick. Fold into egg white mixture by hand or with mixer at lowest speed, fold in 1/2 cup pistachio nuts.

Spoon into baked shell.

Sprinkle with crumbs.

Freeze until firm, 4 to 6 hours; cover.

James R. Thompson
Governor, Illinois

Dark Mocha Cake

5 oz. bitter chocolate, cubed
1/2 cup milk
1 cup sugar
1 egg yolk
1/2 tsp. salt
1/4 cup water
1/2 cup milk
1 tsp. vanilla
3 egg whites
1/2 cup butter
1 cup light brown sugar
2 egg yolks
2 cups cake flour
1 tsp. baking soda

In saucepan combine bitter chocolate and 1/2 cup milk. Stir over low heat until chocolate is melted and mixture is smooth. Stir in the one cup of sugar and one egg yolk. Cook, stirring constantly, for three minutes, or until custard is thick and smooth. Cool.

Cream the 1/2 cup butter until soft. Gradually add light brown sugar; cream together until mixture is light and smooth. Beat in two egg yolks, one at a time.
Sift and measure cake flour. Resift with baking soda and salt. Add to butter mixture in three parts, alternately with the water, remaining 1/2 cup milk and teaspoon of vanilla. Stir in custard.

Beat egg whites until stiff, but not dry, and fold into cake batter. Divide batter into two buttered nine-inch layer cake pans and bake in a pre-heated 375 degree oven for 25-30 minutes, or until layers test done.

Turn cakes out onto racks to cool, then put together with French coffee icing. Frost top lavishly, or frost top and sides smoothly with remaining icing.

French Coffee Icing

1 cup butter
1/4 teaspoon salt
2 Tbls. instant coffee
1 tsp. rum
4 Tbls. boiling water
2-1/2 cups unsifted confectioners sugar

Beat butter until soft; add salt and the instant coffee which has been dissolved in the boiling water.

Gradually add unsifted confectioners sugar. Beat for two minutes. Add rum and allow to stand for five minutes, then beat again.

Gov. Lamar Alexander
Tennessee

Sour Cream Cake

1 cup sour cream
1 cup sugar
Cream together well
Add
2 eggs, beaten
1 tsp. soda in water
1/2 Tbs. cocoa
1-1/4 cup flour
1 tsp. vanilla

Combine all ingredients and put in 9x11x2 lightly greased pan. Bake 350 degrees 25 minutes or until done to test.

This is David Janssen's favorite cake.

Berniece Janssen
Ziegfeld Girl

"There are two types of men in the world that I feel sincerely sorry for. One is the fellow that thinks he knows women and the other is the one that is always saying 'I know the Mississippi River.'"

Chocolate Custard Sponge Pudding

2 Squares unsweetened chocolate
2 Cups milk
4 Tablespoon flour
1/2 Cup sugar
1/4 Teaspoon salt
2 Tablespoon melted butter
3 Eggs seperated
1-1/2 Teaspoon vanilla or peppermint flavoring

Chop chocolate and add to milk in top of a double boiler. Heat over boiling water until chocolate is melted. Beat with rotary beater until smooth. Combine with flour, sugar, and salt. Add butter and mix well. Blend in egg yolks, add hot chocolate mix gradually blend well. Add vanilla. Beat egg whites until they stand in soft peaks, fold into chocolate mixture. Turn into a 8 inch square baking dish. Place 8 inch pan in a larger pan with hot water added. Bake in a pre-heated 350° oven 45 minutes or until custard is set. Serve warm or cold. Makes 6 to 8 servings.

Marjorie Hansen
Docent, Will Rogers State Park

Coconut Macaroons

1-1/4 Cups butter
1 Cup sugar
1 Cup brown sugar, firmly packed
2 Eggs, beaten
2-1/4 Cups sifted flour
1/3 Teaspoon baking soda
2 Teaspoons baking powder
1/2 Teaspoon salt
1 Cup rolled oats
1 Cup chopped nuts
2 Cups coconut
1 Tablespoon orange extract

Cream butter until fluffy, add sugars, cream until light and fluffy. Beat in eggs. Stir dry ingredients into creamed mixture. Add last three ingredients. Mix well, Roll dough into balls about the size of a walnut. Place on an ungreased cookie sheet about three inches apart. Bake 12 to 15 minutes, or until golden brown. Bake in a preheated 350° oven.

Kathy Holt
Park Maintenance Worker 1

Strawberries and Custard Sauce

Wash and hull 2 quarts of berries and drain. Put in bowl and chill. Pour off any water and spread 2 cups strawberry jam thinned with 1/4 cup Kirsch over berries and serve with custard sauce.

CUSTARD SAUCE
In the top of double boiler, scald 1 cup heavy cream and stir in 2 Tbsp. sugar. Beat 4 egg whites with another cup of heavy cream and warm this mixture with a little of the hot cream. Stir well and gradually add all of this to hot cream. Set pan over boiling water and cook custard, stirring constantly until thick. Stir in 1 tsp. vanilla. Pour into glass jar, cover and chill. (This custard sauce will keep for a long time in the refrigerator, and is delicious over other types of berries, too.)

Pierre du Pont
Governor of Delaware

Strawberry Shortcake

2 Angel Food cakes
3 8 oz. containers frozen strawberries
2 pints of whipping cream
4 T. sugar

Tear or cut angel food cake into bite size pieces and place a layer in a 13x9″ Pyrex dish. Defrost strawberries and place in blender until well blended. Whip cream until light and fluffy, gradually adding sugar. Pour half of strawberry mixture over angel food cake, press down with a fork and cover with half of whipped cream. Repeat three layers once more. Garnish with whole strawberries, if possible. Serves about 8.

If you are ever in the State of Mississippi, please come by and visit with us here at the Governor's Mansion.

Cliff Finch
Governor of Mississippi

The Cookies

2 cubes butter (1/2 pound)
1/2 Cup sugar
1 egg, beaten
2-1/2 Cups flour
1-1/4 Cup oatmeal

Melt the butter, add sugar and beaten egg, mix well, add the flour, mix well, add the oatmeal, mix well. Using three 10x15 cookie sheets, put 1/3 of the dough on each pan. Cover dough with saran wrap, so the dough will not stick to whatever you are going to roll it out with. (I use a round spice jar.) Remove the saran wrap. With a knife crease the dough in the pan to the size you want the cookies to be. Bake in a pre-heated 350° oven,watching that the cookies do not get to dark. Let cool on a rack and enjoy. These cookies are never fail. You do not touch them with your hands until they are ready to eat. They take about one half an hour from start to finish, enjoy

Peno and Nora Dwinger

INDEX

Appetizers
  Beans and Chili, 44
  Cheese Ring, Plains Special, 165
  Irish Coffee O'Callaghan Style, 164
  Liver Pate, 164
  Mike's Mushrooms, 166
  Razmatasle, 163
  Tomato Juice Cocktail, 163

Beef
  (B and O) Railroad Stew, 56
  Beef, Cold Platter, 93
  Brisket, Barbecued, 40
  California Chili, 55
  Chili, Julian's, 67
  Corned Beef and Cabbage a la Dinty
    Moore, 25
  Cowboy Casserole, 107
  Hamburger Casserole, 113
  Hamburger, Italian Delight, 133
  Hamburger, Minestrone, 175
  Hamburger Pie, 98
  Hamburger Torte 'Tijuana', 85
  Herb's Chili Recipe, 92
  Hungarian Beef, 82
  Hungarian Goulash with Noodles, 70
  Lasagna, 59
  "More's" One Dish Dinner, 99
  Rice Dressing, 71
  Rice Hot Dish,Wild, 76
  Rouladen, 42
  Sarma, 50
  Sauerbraten, 79
  Spaghetti, 119
  Spaghetti Western, 120
  Swedish Meatballs, quick, 54
  Tenderloin, 38
  Tequila Fajitas, 81
  Teriyaki, 62
  Tortilla, Layered, 63
  Western Barbequed Burgers, 53
Beverage
  Irish Coffee, 164
  Tomato Juice Cocktail, 163

Bread
  Banana Bread, 221
  Banana Nut Bread, 189
  Basic Sourdough Recipe, 182
  Corn Meal Pancakes, 191
  Corn, Hot Water, 183
  Florida Orange Bread, 186
  Hot Water Cornbread, 183
  Jane and Dicks Popovers, 188
  Leola's Cornbread, 185
  Self Rising Bread, 187
  Squaw Bread, 183
  Will Rogers Centennial Corn Bread, 190
  Zucchini Date/Nut Bread, 184

Cake
  Apple Cake, 232
  Banana Cake, 196
  Banana Split Cake, 258
  Betty's Cherry Nut Cake, 227
  Carrot Cake, 220
  Carrot Pineapple Cake, 209
  Chocolate Buttermilk Cake, 215
  Coconut Pound Cake, 214
  Dark Mocha Cake, 260
  F.R.F.'S Southern Delight, 238
  Hasty Cake, 246
  Hummingbird Cake, 229
  Maggi Cake, 210
  Mertz Poor Man's Cake, 236
  Oatmeal Cake, 218
  Oklahoma Crude Cake, 231
  Oma Cake, 211
  Pumpkin Cake, 239
  Southern Red Velvet Cake, 234
  Sour Cream Cake, 262
  Strawberry Shortcake, 265
  Virginia Apple Cake, 213
  Walnut Torte, 243
  Wine Cake, 219
Casseroles
  Baked Beans, 125
  Cheese Strata, 123
  Chicken Casserole, 118

Corn and Oyster, 114
Corn Pudding, 134
Cowboy Casserole, 107
Eggplant Supreme, 127
Garden Pizza, 117
Green Bean Casserole, 128
Hamburger Casserole, 113
Ham Strata, 112
Italian Delight, 133
Macaroni and Cheese Casserole, 110
Mandarin Drumsticks, 108
Noodle Pudding, 111
Potato and Onion Casserole, 124
Quiche Lorraine, 130
Savory Sausage, 122
Spaghetti Casserole, 119
Spaghetti Western, 120
Spareribs and Sauerkraut, 121
Spinach Casserole, 109
Spinach Ring, 106
Sunday Dinner, 121
Sweet Potato Casserole, 131
Zucchini Casserole, 116

Cheese
Cheese Casserole and Macaroni, 110
Cheese Sauce and Eggs, 45
Cheese Strata, 123
Quiche Lorraine, 130
Quick Quiche, 74

Chili
California Chili, 55
Chili and Beans, 44
Chili Pie, 49
Herb's Chili Recipe, 92
Julian's Chili, 67

Cookies
Aunt Freda's Peanut Butter Cookies, 249
Coconut Macaroons, 264
Dodi's Whoopie Pies, 248
Grandma Zimmerman's Sour Cream
  Cookies, 206
Molasses Cookies, 217
Old Fashion Sugar Cookies, 251
Oldtime Cinnamon Jumbles, 252

Ranger Cookies, 223
Spider Cookies, 228
The Cookies, 266
Walnut Meringues, 241
Wonder Cookies, 221

Desserts
Caramel Custard, 204
Carrot Pudding, 253
Centennial Luncheon Apple Crisp, 254
Chocolate Custard Sponge Pudding, 263
Chocolate Ice Box Dessert, 235
Chocolate Nut Bars, 256
Coffee Ice Cream, 256
Cranberry Crunch, 208
English Trifle, 207
Favorite Ice Cream, 233
French Coffee Icing, 261
Fresh Peach Ice Cream, 203
Fudgey Brownies, 228
Lemon Squares, 226
Lemon Squares, 237
Lorie's Grasshopper Desert, 245
Moose Meat Mince Meat, 197
Norma Stouffer's Quick Lemon
  Crisps, 216
Old Fashion Hot Fudge Sauce, 212
Ozark Pudding, 247
Peach-Berry Cobbler, 199
Peach Ice cream, 247
Plum Pudding, 250
Pots de Creme, 233
Pots De Creme De Chocolate, 230
Rodgers Dodger's Dutch Baby, 240
Scottish Scones, 202
Strawberries and Custard Sauce, 265
Strawberry Roll Supreme, 257
Sugar Surprise, 222

Eggs
Eggs American Indian Style and
  Wild Onions, 35
Eggs and Wild Onions, 48
Egg Timbales with Cheese Sauce, 45

Fish
Baked Snapper with Crab Meat,

Mousseline Sauce, 36
Baked Stuffed Shrimp, 61
Barbecued Trout, 87
Bay Country Crab Soup, 178
California Shrimp with Mandarin
  Oranges, 155
Clam Chowder, 176
Cocktail Sauce with Avocados, 138
Crab Imperial, 95
Crab Quiche, 31
Governor Ray's All Time Favorite
  Bouillabaisse, 68
Gumbo, 172
Lobster Ragout, 65
Marie Spota's Lemon Fish or Chicken, 75
Mousse of Sole with Hollandaise, 39
Oysters and Corn, 114
Paella Amigos, 32
Salmon Patties and Potato Patches, 129
Seafood a la Newberg, 72
Seasoning for Fish Etc., 80
Shrimp Salad, 143
Souffle de Saumon, 102

Fowl
  Baked Chicken Hollandaise, 60
  Chicken Almond, 52
  Chicken Cacciatora, 41
  Chicken Casserole, 118
  Chicken Enchiladas Babbitt, 66
  Chicken Fruit Salad, 149
  Chicken Supreme, 83
  Estelle's Chicken, 28
  Joe's Fried Chicken, 78
  Larry Beye's Chicken Salad, 148
  Lorri's Sunday Supper, 121
  Mandarin Drumsticks, 108
  Marie Spota's Lemon Chicken, 75
  Roast Duck with Sausage Stuffing, 101
  Roast Pheasant, 77
  Sesame Seed Chicken Wings, 94
  Sherried Chicken, 29
  Sweet and Sour Chicken, 98
Pies
  Cafe's Pecan Pumpkin Pie and
    Carmel Sauce, 242

Chili Pie, 49
Maudie Dumas' Fresh Fruit Pie, 201
New Hampshire Wild Blueberry Pie, 198
Nutty Fudge Pie, 255
Pecan Pie, 200
Pistachio Pie, 259
Pumpkin Pie, 195
Tortilla Pie, 63

Pork
  Baked Pork Chops, 46
  Ham Loaf, 47
  Ham Strata, 112
  Impossible Quiche, 90
  Roast Loin of Pork/Orange Sauce with
    Almond Stuffed Onions, 88
  Sarma, 50
  Sausage Stuffing with Roast Duck, 101
  Sausage with Potato Soup, 177
  Savory Sausage, 122
  Spareribs and Sauerkraut, 121
  Spiced Apple Pork Roast, 100
  Stuffed Ham Seville, 64

Salads
  24-Hour Salad, 142
  Avocado Salad, 150
  Avocado with Hot Cocktail Sauce, 138
  Beye's Chicken Salad, 148
  Chicken Fruit Salad, 149
  Cottage Cheese Jello Salad, 144
  Cucumber and Pineapple Salad, 144
  Grandpa's Salad Dressing, 140
  Shrimp Salad, 143
  Shrimp Salad, 145
  Spinach Salad, 147
  "Steves" Potato Salad, 146
  Tapioca Salad, 141
  Three Rice-Walnut Salad, 139
  Vermicelli Salad, 145

Sauces
  Cowboy Dip, 158
  Grandpa's Guacamole, 157
  "It's the Pits Of Claremore" Salsa, 154
  Wilder Ranch Fiesta Salsa, 156

270

Soups
  Bean Soup, 171
  Clam Chowder, 176
  Corn Chowder, 174
  Crab Soup, 178
  Creme Senegalaise, 170
  Gumbo, 172
  Hamburger Minestrone Soup, 175
  Potato Soup with Sausage, 177
  Steak Soup, 97

Veal
  Veal New Mexico, 43
  Veal Scaloppine, 84

Vegetables
  Almond Stuffed Onions, 88
  Baked Beans, 125
  "Barba Giuan", 126
  Bean Soup, 171
  Black Beans NY/TX Style, 96
  Buddy Rogers Eggplant Supreme, 127
  Corn and Oysters, 114
  Corn Chowder, 174
  Corn Pudding, 134
  Eggplant Palmagiano, 91
  Eggplant Stew, 86

Farcis, 115
Garden Pizza, 117
Green Bean Casserole, 128
Joel McCrea Beans, 27
Mike's Mushrooms, 166
Mrs. Rogers Green Beans, 57
Mushrooms, 51
Peppers and Franks, 73
Potato Patches, 129
Potato Salad, 146
Potato Soup, 177
Potato Supreme, 34
"Pure Oklahoma" Squaw Corn, 114
Sauerkraut, 121
Scalloped Potatoes and Onions, 124
Spinach, 147
Spinach Balls, 132
Spinach Casserole, 109
Spinach Ring, 106
Sweet Potato, 131
Wild Onions, 48
Wild Onions and Eggs, 35
Will Rogers Beans, 58
Zucchini, 116
Zucchini, 184

271